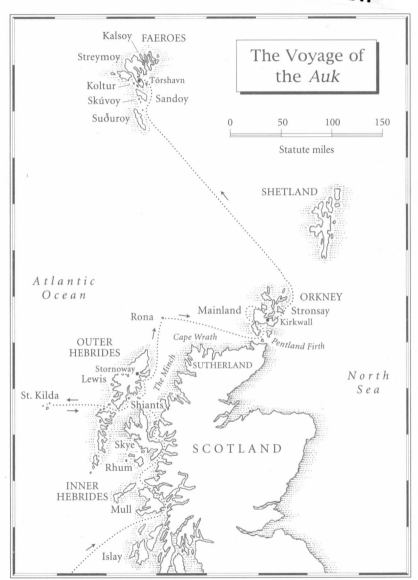

Kalsoy FAEROES
Streymoy
Koltur Tórshavn
Skúvoy Sandoy
Suðuroy

The Voyage of the *Auk*

0   50   100   150

Statute miles

SHETLAND

Atlantic Ocean

Rona Mainland ORKNEY
Cape Wrath Stronsay
Kirkwall
Pentland Firth

OUTER HEBRIDES
Stornoway SUTHERLAND
Lewis

North Sea

St. Kilda
Shiants

Skye SCOTLAND

Rhum

INNER HEBRIDES
Mull

Islay

SEAMANSHIP

SEAMANSHIP

*A Voyage
Along the Wild Coasts
of the British Isles*

A<small>DAM</small> N<small>ICOLSON</small>

HarperCollins*Publishers*

HarperCollins books may be purchased for educational, business, or sales promotional use. For information, please write: Special Markets Department, HarperCollins Publishers Inc., 10 East 53rd Street, New York, NY 10022.

First published in Great Britain in 2004 by HarperCollins Publishers.

FIRST EDITION

Endpaper map by John Gilkes

Printed on acid-free paper

Library of Congress Cataloging-in-Publication Data
Nicolson, Adam.
    Seamanship : a voyage along the wild coasts of the British Isles / Adam Nicolson.—1st U.S. ed.
      p. cm.
    ISBN 0-06-075342-0
    1. Great Britain—Description and travel. 2. Nicolson, Adam.—Travel—Great Britain. 3. Navigation—Great Britain. 4. Coasts—Great Britain. I. Title.
DA632.N53 2005
910'.9163'37—dc22   2004054014

05 06 07 08 09 RPTUK/RRD 10 9 8 7 6 5 4 3 2 1

For Sarah

SEAMANSHIP

1

The *Auk*

I was having an affair with the Atlantic. Alone with my books in my room, I had been thinking of little else for weeks. I was longing for the sea. I wanted to get out, away from my desk, into the air, somewhere on the big Atlantic shore of the British Isles, that incomparable, islanded world which has more miles of coastline than the whole eastern seaboard of the United States. Not just to see it, but to sail it, to immerse myself in that ocean side of the country, its long, beautiful wildness, from headland to headland, the place where high winds met hard rock. I wanted days and nights of it. If I thought of openness, or even freedom, it was the Atlantic that filled my mind. I didn't mention it to Sarah. I knew these were, in their heart, treacherous thoughts.

I went down, one Sunday, to the beach on the

Sussex coast. Milky rollers poured on to the shingle. The café windows stared at them as though the sea weren't there. People sat in their cars looking at the waves. From time to time they used their wipers to clear their windscreens of the spray. I drank it in and felt stranded on the shore. To be out there! What would I give for that?

Until the eighteenth century, Europeans thought the sea in general and beaches in particular smelled disgusting. The air on a beach was not full of life-restoring, energising ozone, but stiff with rot. The beach was where the natural order collapsed and the sea beyond it was pure anarchy. It carried no marks of history or civilisation and was filled with nauseating monsters whose flesh turned putrid if ever cast ashore. When, in the first chapter of Genesis, the Spirit of God was said to move 'upon the face of the waters', those waters were clearly what God was not. The sea was the absence of all meaning, not its source.

But I wasn't living in 1680, I was heir to another tradition. Looking out from the beach suggested to me, as it had to others for two or three hundred years, something larger than the ordinariness of life on land. The Romantic instinct equates roughness with reality.

It thinks of the sheer discomfort and violence of the sea as the guarantee of authenticity, the lack of safety a measure, strangely, of truth.

It is a curious fact that you can know why you are acting as you are; be fully aware of the influences which have you in their grasp; understand the damage which those actions might cause; and still be unable to do anything about it. So I talked to Sarah one evening. 'The sea?' she said, a sudden focus in her eyes. Yes, yes, I explained, the sea, the western shore, that wild place, away from here, encountering the world as it was, a boat, perhaps from March to October.

She looked away and said, 'If that is what you need to do, that is what you need to do. But you have got to make sure we are all right here before you go.' She took the idea for what it was, a kind of leaving, a desire to live before you die. 'I don't want you to go,' she said, 'but I can't stop you.'

Alone with an atlas and a cup of coffee, I picked a course, wandering through that ocean-enriched and ocean-threatened world. Not knowing what I wanted or needed, I looked at yachts in magazines. Nor, to be honest, did I know how to sail. I knew the rudiments but little else and had little seacraft, the half-instinctive knowledge of what to do when things go wrong. Blindly, I found a man in the phone book who said he was an expert and drove down to Brighton to see him. It was the first lesson in seamanship. Everything I had been dreaming of, the whole inflated soufflé, collapsed on sight. His yacht, something called a Bavaria 46, tied up in the marina, was a big fat white empty plastic thing, a bulbous caravan with too many cabins and no soul. My heart sank. And sank further as the man told me how he'd been in the RAF, how this was a cushy number for him, as if the sea was part of the saloon bar, its surface coated in swirly floral carpet, the red cherries on sticks. 'It's no more difficult to learn than golf,' he said, 'easier in many respects.' He had never been to the west coast of Ireland.

I was flummoxed. At home that evening, Sarah – and this was a measure of her strength of mind – said, 'Why not ring George Fairhurst?' I hadn't spoken to him in years, scarcely since we had been sailing together off the coast of the Algarve. But of course he was the man: still in his early forties but a skipper of immense, ocean-going experience, with half a million sea miles under his belt, who had skippered square-sail ships and taken sail-training vessels across the Atlantic, to the Caribbean and back, up the coast of America; an Ocean Yachtmaster, a qualified Yachtmaster Instructor. But more than that, he was quite clearly a man who understood that the sea and sailing were more than just another version of golf, not just another play zone, but a way of being alive. I remembered something he had said to me one night when we were halfway to Ireland with the stars above us, some words from a film, the visions from a sea journey that would be 'lost in time, like tears in rain . . .'

Years ago, he had taught me, more or less, how to sail a yacht and now, perhaps, on this six-month journey from the spring to the autumn equinox, he might teach me again, in a bigger boat in bigger seas, how to be there, how to sail, how to cope.

I rang him on his mobile. He was in the pub in Falmouth. He had just been sailing all day, a big roaring trip up the Channel with some friends. The noise of the pub behind him. I could see his listening face. Did he know of anyone who might come with me on this trip up the Atlantic shore? Who might teach me to sail an ocean-going boat over the course of the year? Who could help me find a boat? Who would be a sympathetic companion with reserves of sea-understanding on which we could draw when things turned for the worst?

He did. No hesitation. He would come. It would be a thing to have done on which the rest of his life could feed. 'When do we begin?'

'Well, we need a boat, George.'

'I'll start looking tomorrow.'

The right kind of boat needed to be quite big, forty to forty-two foot, to deal with the Atlantic, particularly as the swells came unbroken on to the west coast of Ireland. No bigger because that would become difficult with just the two of us. It needed a meaty engine as well as good new sails to get out of problems. It shouldn't be one of those elegant New England yachts with long counter sterns and overhanging bows – sleek, leggy supermodels – because they were not made for the big seas that would be our world. She would have to be strong, beamy, and secure. She might not be the fastest, but we could live with that.

We looked for weeks. We toured the harbours and boatyards of England. We scoured the magazines and had sessions on the Internet. There were phone conversations with boat owners in California and Maine. Something for a while looked right in Bergen. But everything had its flaws. Perhaps I didn't entirely know what I wanted in the way of a boat. George walked me round marinas. Did I like the look of that kind of thing? Or that? Was that too flash? Or that too slick? Too big? Too small? Too fat? Too thin? Too little headroom below? Too ugly? Too pretentious? Too sharky? Too cute?

We had by now reached the middle of November. Time was running on and the boat, the right boat, still wasn't showing up. Then, late one evening, George rang me from his mobile. 'I'm on her,' he said.

'Why are you whispering?'

'I've crept aboard. I've found the hatch open. There's no one here and I'm sitting below and this is the boat. I think this is the one.'

I was down there the next morning at dawn, to a marina at Lymington on the Solent. Plastic decks, hi-tech rigs, and long sleek windows like the lenses of wrap-around shades spread around me in aprons of money. But over on a far pontoon, sticking up amid the aluminium, I saw a pair of wooden masts. George was poking around at the base of one of them. There she was. She lay in her skimpy little pontoon berth like a duchess in a supermarket, scarcely deigning to consider the indignity of her surroundings. Immensely wooden, larch planks on oak frames, superbly fat around the middle, with volumes of room below, enough berths to sleep eight, the perfect candidate, a substance in her big rounded stem and stern. She was descended, via a good few cream cakes, from the sailing lifeboats of nineteenth-century Norway, designed by the great naval architect Colin Archer – his parents were Scottish – to be safe in a storm. Her forebears had been built to wait offshore in the North Sea and, as bad weather struck, to take fishing boats in tow and claw off a lee shore, holding them like a gaggle of ducklings behind them. She was the kind of boat Erskine Childers used to run guns to the IRA in the Irish Civil War – her innards stripped out below and filled with a glittering pool of rifles. She was as strong as you like and only fourteen years old, built as an apprentice piece in a yard at Heiligenhafen on the Baltic. Here was the boat for the ocean margin. She exuded certainty. She would look after us. She was the one. She was one of us.

Staring down at her I couldn't quite believe such

a thing might ever be mine. Such a ship! It was as if I had given birth to a cow. I negotiated a mortgage with Barclays Marine Finance, offered two-thirds of the asking price, subject to sea trial and survey, and it was accepted.

Early in December, I drove down in the dawn to a freezing Lymington. The wind was gusting up to thirty knots, a Force 7. With the ship broker, all courtesy, all smoothing of every path, and an employee of the owner who had been out on the boat before, we edged into the winter sea. We soon had all four sails up – a genoa, a staysail, the mainsail, and the mizzen – and she went, steadily, rather like a drawing room afloat, no huge speed, but so homely, with such a big calm motion, sailing at six or seven knots or so in the Solent, kettle on the gimballed cooker, that there were smiles all round.

The boat needed setting up properly. The shrouds, the big stays for the mast, were not in the right place and as a result the mainmast leaned forward slightly. The sheetleads and blocks were all wrong. The mainsheet arrangement was a chaos. The sails were both too small and too loose, and she was underpowered.

For all that, there was something there, the sense of

what might be. The yacht that windy morning felt like a capsule of possibilities. A boat is not a destination, nor a conclusion, as a house or a piece of land might be, but a means to reach conclusions and destinations that otherwise you could only dream of. Everything that hangs in the air above a boat is open-ended. She knows no horizons. For her, anyway, every prospect is an invitation and every casting-off an absorption in where she might go. A boat is all beginnings, and something about that boat that morning felt as if she wanted to go, to head out there and get out there, to sail out into the sea for which she had been made.

There was a moment when George and I both lay down on our backs on the foredeck, looking up at the mast and headsails while the big girl rumbled along beneath us in the wind. That was also a beginning, as if we were astronauts lined up on the pad.

Later, in the pub at Lymington, George allowed himself to talk about what we might do, where we might go, what the year might mean. A mission, he called it, and was clearly touched by it, by the things we would see, the whales surfacing at night, the phosphorescence running off the bow, the early mornings, the harbours after storms.

All that open-endedness requires the very opposite from the boat itself. The boat needed to be closed. The Atlantic shore is the realm of possibilities, but if this boat was to thrive there she needed to sharpen up. George had already shown a photograph of her in her current state to a boatbuilder in Cornwall – her short masts, leaning forward, her baggy, tiny sails, her unachieved condition. 'Oh, look at her,' the Cornishman had said, 'broken wings.' If she was to be released into her Atlantic life, she had to be redeemed and to do that we would have to take her down-Channel to the Cornish yard. And, despite the superstitions, give her a new name. She was called *Irene May* when I bought her, after the mother of the previous owner, but that couldn't stay. George's own mother, Bar, understanding these things, and seeing a picture of her, thought she might be renamed the *Auk*, because her big round body and her slightly stumpy wings reminded her of the way the auks – the razorbills and guillemots and puffins – all exist so bravely and buoyantly in their gale-swept oceanic world. The auk is the bird of the ocean and it was as the *Auk* that we finally took her to sea.

Negotiations over the price and conditions of the

sale had run on – there had been problems with the masts – and it was early February by the time she was released to go. A hundred and fifty miles of the winter sea, a huge lump of sea life taken in at a gulp. George had driven up from Cornwall to Lymington and spent the night on her. I drove down in another dawn. Anxious excitement, a boat we didn't know, big south-south-westerlies coming across the Channel. A long hike in February, hard on the wind, with certainly no other yacht at sea, one of us as green as they come, the other at least a little rusty. Getting things ready in the early dark, eggs and bacon down below, saying we would just go out into the Solent to start with, just to test the gear, to see how the newly fixed rigging would perform, not entirely certain that the engine was in the greatest of shapes. But knowing, somehow, that there was a big draw out there – that invitation westwards, down the Channel.

I was fingers and thumbs. I scarcely knew a knot that was any good. I hadn't yet grasped that running a boat involved sweat and physical engagement. It doesn't happen while sipping a glass of white wine. We reattached the big genoa in the morning to the forestay while the wind flogged and snatched at it. I made a mess of it three times before George stepped in. We fuelled up. The man operating the pump said, 'So you're the fellow who bought dear old *Irene May*? She's built like a horse, isn't she?'

Was that good? Was a horse what you wanted? I'd no idea.

We left eventually in the early afternoon. The marvellous abandonment of leaving. The wind still coming in sharply up the Channel as we headed out under the motor. Sick with apprehension and strangeness. The tide just short of the Needles was kicking up into little pinnacles. I would have been swamped or capsized in any dinghy, but the *Auk* slapped through it all, the sunshine off the milky water, the headlands stepping away to the southwest. We hauled up the mainsail and set the genoa in what had by then turned into big heaving seas, the bow plunging in as the *Auk* took each new one. George went below, leaving me at the wheel. Two things happened at once: the full whack of a bigger-than-average wave came all the way back to the cockpit, a freezing, drenching, dense, heavy shower that left me with a face aching like a mouth that has had too much ice cream; and I threw up over the lee side-deck.

It was like a sneeze – a clean, straight, if enormous, expulsion; everything from breakfast onwards, leaving me surprised to have been that sick that quickly. George came up from below with a cup of tea. I drank that and sicked it up. Then a couple of chocolate biscuits that went the same yo-yo route. I saw a look of resigned horror on George's face. At that time of year, the night lasts about fourteen hours, from five in the afternoon to about seven in the morning. He had an invalid along with him. How was he going to manage it?

The rest of the voyage remains what can only be called impressionistic. Sick every now and then, cheerful enough to start with but gradually shrinking into a little ball of cold and paralysis. George saying, 'You have got to keep moving.' Me, ignorant of everything around me – boat, sea, systems, methods, means of keeping well – shrivelling with what felt like straightforward shutdown but was perhaps fear. 'Why don't we just go into Weymouth?' I said to George, longing for some relief. 'Better to go on,' he said. 'We'll have eighty miles under our belt tomorrow.' Shrunken child of a passenger, I said yes, was sick, crept down to my sleeping bag in the saloon, sick on the way down, sick as I took off my oilies, sick getting into the sleeping bag, sick every now and then into a bucket George had put beside me. It was 5.15 in the afternoon and it felt like midnight.

From time to time in the night George came down, a huge figure in his wet oilies, reeking of a hellish world outside, to check our course on the instruments below. It was now blowing a full gale, Force 8, and the sea was against us. All I could hear was the grinding and banging of the rig and the heavy bass thumping as the bows fell into each new sea. At one of his visitations I was being sick. 'Everything all right?' he said.

'Fine,' I said. 'Are you OK?'

'Fine, thanks.'

At about one o'clock in the morning, I woke again and felt too ashamed of what was happening, pulled on my clothes and waterproofs, gloves and hat, and went on deck. It was bitterly, bitingly, grippingly cold and the bow was throwing one freezing shower of spray after another the full length of the boat. The deck gleamed green and red with the nav lights. I managed to persuade George that I was feeling all right and he went below for a sleep after more than eight hours at the wheel, half of it in a blizzard in which the rain was ice.

The privacy of the winter sea closes in at night. Far to the south I could see the big pale looms of the lights in the Channel Islands lifting up above the horizon like wraiths. The cold of the night prickled on the skin. England – the yellow lights of its coast roads necklaced in the dark to the north – was a foreign country. Here just the grinding and the thumping of the boat as she pulled her way westwards into the night. Seas came at you blind. There was no reading them. All I could do was drive on into them and take the thump, the shudder, and the cascade as we hit each wall. Fishing boats, lights swinging wildly, crossed our bows and occasionally a tall merchant ship, lit like a Christmas hotel, steamed past at three or four times our speed in the dark.

The hours went by. The sky cleared and the stars emerged. Orion had his legs and feet deep in the western Channel, the horizon sliding up to his waist and down again. Cassiopeia hung and slewed like a windblown billboard in the rigging to my right. I have never been colder in my life. My gloves were wet inside and my fingers didn't feel. George had said, 'You need to be a little more fastidious about your gloves', but I hadn't been and wet, cold fingers were the result. I was still sick from time to time but was fixed on giving George at least four hours of rest. I looked at the lit places ashore and felt no envy. Even in this cold and discomfort I was glad to be here, not inert in my bed, but out in the air, a small unroofed presence in the world, sticking up like a single hair on the world's skin, feeling the atmosphere as a reality around me, and, because of that, somehow deriving reality and substance of my own.

We began to slide and ride the waves, as the longer Atlantic swell started to take up from the shorter Channel chop, a longer, oceanic movement, the under-rhythm of the west. The stars were no longer jerking and jumping around the masts, but swinging their easy dance between them. The big strong boat, so made for this, the ocean horse in her element. For a moment, with no more than a shred of understanding of how to do it, I felt extraordinarily confident, happily riding this thing, at home at sea.

Endless night, the endless looking to the east for a sign of day. None there when, at four o'clock, George came up again, all oiled up, and sent me below.

Instant sleep. Nothing till I heard him shouting: 'Adam! Adam!' I went up. The sunrise was like a barred grey flag in the east. The daylit sea looked old and tired. The wind had dropped, but the water was still broken, like a rough-sawn surface. 'Look, look,' George said as I came up the companionway steps. All around us were porpoises, forty or fifty of them, surging freedom after the prison of the night, the gleam on their backs stained orange by the sun.

George made me asparagus soup, warm and beautiful. I sicked it up. Oatcakes. The same. We slid on, a little dazed, through the morning, the Cornish headlands now in view. 'Would you like to be in Weymouth now?' George asked. No, no. But I felt shaken and exhausted. His face was puffy too, as if beaten. We turned at last into Carrick Roads, the long sleeve of an anchorage on whose shore Falmouth sits. The sea went flat in the shelter and the world quiet. The green sweetness of the woods and fields. We passed two of the Falmouth oystermen, sailing their traditional oyster dredgers in the Roads, boats as fine as curlews, their long bowsprits curved down in front of them, the men at the helm just touching the tiller an inch to catch a gust, tweaking a sheet as if it were needlepoint they were at. I felt as if I had been living inside the head of a sledgehammer.

Kathy Bevan, George's girlfriend, met us on the quay at Mylor and we drank whisky, straight, at eleven in the morning, sitting on board at the saloon table. She looked at us as if we had been in an accident.

'Have you learned anything, Adam?' she said, smiling at me a sweet, warm, womanly harbour-smile. Had I? Perhaps that a storm at night teaches you the beauty of harbours. All the grommets on the mainsail had burst. The planking in the bow, where we had slammed into those big ones, had visibly shifted. I was dazed with the motion and my head still swam. Neither I nor the *Auk* had ever lived like this. It is often said that a man's boat is an extension of himself, but that is not quite true. A man's boat is more an instrument by which his self is exposed.

George remade the *Auk*. She went into the operating theatre and her agony lasted six weeks, drying out in a yard at Tregatreath on Mylor Creek, one of the arms of the sea that reach inland from Carrick Roads. There she leant up against the ragged concrete quay, where only one tide a month comes high enough to float her. Her keel stood on the mud-coated concrete, ladders propped against her, all dignity gone. Rough patches appeared on the hull where the chainplates securing the shrouds were moved. Down below was chaos, all deck-linings off, all bunks and lockers out, tools everywhere, the cabin sole up and the guts of the boat exposed. Poor *Auk*!

Of course, it was for the good. She was to have a new sprayhood, to protect us from seas coming back over the length of the boat, and a teak stopwater to stop those seas running down into the cockpit. The cockpit itself needed new drains; the heads'l winches were to be moved to the side-decks on little purpose-made tables and a new mainsheet winch installed; the mainmast needed more tension and the backstay system had to be improved; there was to be a complete new set of sails, taller and wider than the old set, to power her up; the spars and running rigging had to be adjusted in proportion; a hard dinghy was commissioned for the deck; the interior cushions were re-upholstered; the batteries were re-housed in waterproof casings; more hand-holds were fitted; the deck was treated; and we bought what felt like a large inflatable.

Finally, in mid-March, she was done, or as good

as we would get her. We had sluiced and hoovered every conceivable nook and hollow. She had been honed and tuned. The tide that would float the new *Auk* would reach its peak at three o'clock on the Sunday morning. An easterly had been blowing up the creek all day, pulling at the blue tarpaulin over the cockpit, an endless, morale-sapping snatch-and-release. We were tired and it was a testy time. George, Kathy, and I all slept on the boat that evening and woke at quarter to three.

I lay for a minute listening in my bunk. The *Auk* was rocking, afloat. The tide had crept in with the night, the wind had dropped, and the moon was now laying its own silvery path up the creek. With her engine purring slowly beneath us, the boat nudged into life. I stood on the bowsprit, giving warnings back to George. 'Unlit boat ahead, dead ahead!', 'Buoy on the port bow!'

'Got it,' George murmured back again and again from the wheel. We were quiet apart from those few spoken signals. Kathy sat with George in the cockpit and as we passed the ghost-forms of the moored oyster boats in the night, I felt a kind of release. Out at the Mylor yacht harbour we tied up and the *Auk*, the new

Auk, joggled there slightly in the small easterly chop, was ready to go. We were due to leave for Ireland.

We weren't ready. All next day, and the next, and the next, the preparations continued. We bent on the new sails. They didn't seem to fit, and then they did. The mizzen sheet blocks and cleat were all wrong. The sail covers had been made to the wrong size. The sprayhood, to protect us from seas coming back over the boat, was not going to be done in time. We could live without it. A couple of defunct instruments had to be renewed. Food and drink had to be stowed in one place and then another. The dinghy had to be lashed to the deck, the life raft stowed, the 'grab bags', which we would snatch from the boat if she sank, filled with baked beans and Mars bars, lemonade and bottled water, chocolate, torches, a radio, our passports, spare warm clothes, hats, gloves, all or any of which might be of comfort in a life raft: all this took hour after hour. I scrubbed the decks and hosed out the cockpit. Men in the chandlery said, 'I thought you were going yesterday?'

'So did I,' I said, more than once.

I thought at the time that this getting ready was too much and too long, but I see it differently now.

The nature of the voyage is set before you cast off. A sea passage is shaped by the boat's time attached to the land. Every moment at sea is dependent on, and even twinned to, a moment in harbour. What a boat sails on and in is not only the ocean and the wind but the days, weeks, and months tied up alongside.

Finally, late in the afternoon, grey, windy, and cold, with a gale forecast from the south, we were ready, but we weren't. We needed fuel. We took the *Auk* round to the diesel pontoon. George and I were already dressed for sea, in full oilskins, with life jackets and lifelines around our necks, hats and gloves on for the cold. The long tense days of getting ready were visible on George's face, as they must have been on mine. The forecast was bad. A man with his hands in his pockets on the pontoon told me he had gone to Scilly for the last twelve summers, but he wasn't going today. No one in their right mind would go with a forecast like this. 'Really?' I said. 'I think we're going.' I couldn't dream of not going now.

The boy at the diesel pumps – he must have been about nineteen, in his shore anorak, a shock of hair – suddenly said, 'I wish I was coming.' He looked surprised as the words came out of his mouth, too much honesty in a rush. I looked at him and saw myself in him, a man who all his life has stood on the quayside and watched other men going to sea, seeing in them the air of – what is it? Engagement? A task to which they are fully and wholly committed absorbing every part of them? People who are simply deciding to cast off, to go, to leave the here to find the there?

'Come on then,' I said, 'why don't you come? Come now. We've got waterproofs for you, and plenty of food. We're going to Ireland. We should do it in about forty hours with a wind like this. You could be back by the weekend.'

He hesitated. 'Come on,' I said, and stretched my hand out over the gap between the boat and the pontoon. He hung there for a moment, like a diver on the lip, or a fledgling on the verge of leaving the nest, a millimetre difference between staying and going, but then, a flicker of the needle, he held back. 'No, no,' he said. 'I've got too much on here. I can't. I can't. I will, one day. I'm going sailing this summer. Good luck, though! Good luck!'

2

The Passage

I hauled the warps inboard, and as George took the boat under motor out from the quay, I coiled them and stowed them in the starboard cockpit locker. Fenders in and stowed in the lazarette. Stays'l out of its bag, hanked on to the forestay, its tack fitted with a locking shackle to a strop fixed to the stemhead, the head of the sail itself on to the halyard snap-shackle, the tail of the halyard made up on the pin-rail, and the body of the sail marlin-hitched for the time being to the boat's safety rail. The two stays'l sheets then tied with bowlines through the cringle at the clew, led back through the sheet-leads on the side-decks, figure-of-eight stop-knots put into their bitter ends, and the full length of the sheets wound around the secondary winches beside the cockpit.

The mains'l next. Ease the leeward running

backstay and make it off on the leeward shrouds under the light box. Bring the windward backstay up around the primary winch on that side and winch it iron-tight. Release the sail ties holding the mains'l to the gaff and stow them. Unloop the peak and throat halyards from the pin-rail, loosen the leeward topping lift, bring the head of the boat almost up to the wind, ease the main-sheet and haul on both the halyards. Up the sail goes, filling as she does so, that full belly swollen with wind. Make sure the battens in the leach don't get caught on the topping lifts and when they are clear tighten up the throat first and then the peak, making up the main halyards on the rail and then, with the jiggers on the port side, put extra tension into both of them, the luff board-hard, the peak just tight enough to put a crease into the sail running diagonally all the way across it down to the tack. The mizzen up in the same way, then the big heads'l, the high-cut yankee, unravelled from its roller-furling gear on the bowsprit forestay, its leeward sheet hauled in tight on the primary winch next to the cockpit. Finally, the stays'l, released from its marlin-hitched tie, sheets eased, hoisted on its own halyard, made up at the pin-rail, jigged with its own jigger and its leeward sheet winched in on the leeward secondary. Ten minutes out of Mylor, the engine off, a full suit of sails driving her, tell-tales aligned on the swell of the yankee, the *Auk* was now making for Ireland.

In the end, however perfect your boat, you go to sea exhausted, when the weather is least suitable. You just bite off what you can't do. The *Auk* was now going to look after us in a way that before we had only been looking after her. It's the deal you make with your boat. Pour it into her and she will, in time, pour it out for you.

There was a problem. The wind was strong but at least in our favour, just veering that evening from easterly to southerly as we made our way down to the Lizard. If we were lucky it would stay on the beam all the way to Ireland. The boat felt sleek and tight. George and I were tired but keyed up. It then slowly became clear to us that no instruments were working. We turned every switch but nothing came on. The electrician who had arrived to replace two of them two days before did not have a depth gauge in stock. He was going to send it to us in Ireland. But the system on which the instruments worked was an integrated one and no depth gauge in the system meant no readings from anything: no depth of course, no wind speed, no wind direction, no boat speed, no speed over the ground, no course made good, no electronic compass. There was also no light in the magnetic compass and no autohelm. We would have to stand at the wheel, watch and watch about, three or four hours on, three or four hours off, no breaks while you were up there, for the forty hours or so it was going to take us to cross the wide open reach of the Atlantic known as the Celtic Sea.

Driving down south, the sea began to lift under us. We passed the famous Manacles Buoy, marking the killer rocks off the Cornish coast, on which the bell clangs lugubriously day and night, day and night, like a graveyard sexton of the deep. As we passed near enough to read the word 'MANACLE' painted on its vast metal body, George said, 'That bell will still be ringing when we are up in Donegal, or in Orkney, when we are out at sea in the worst storm you have ever known. And it's been ringing these last ten years, for as long and anywhere you have ever been.'

It felt as if we were pushing our fingers deep into the dark. No instruments, no autohelm, no compass light, both of us tired, the boat on her first day out from a refit. We would have to use a hand-held torch to read the bearing on the compass, to align the boat on her distant destination, one of those blessed harbours in the southwest of Ireland, Baltimore or Schull or Crookhaven, a good 250 miles from here. It was a four-way meeting: ocean, boat, me and George, a test set by the first for the other three.

The Lizard light loomed through the thickening dark. We stayed a mile off the headland but still the sea was roughened by the tide, full of huge barn-door breakers. They were coming at us, the whole of the bow plunging into them, burying the bowsprit up to its socket, and the bulk of water driving back along the deck. The spray was lit in the nav lights on either side in huge green arcs of red and green water. There was no sprayhood and every second or two the water burst and rattled on to our waterproofs as the boat plunged on. 'Brave' George called her then. The night was clear and phosphorescence was sprinkled down to leeward like a reflection of the stars. The *Auk* was passing her exam.

'Go down,' George said to me and I slunk down into the safety of the bunk, away from this, sleep instant and deep. No thought for the man on deck and the rattling of the seas as they came over him. Just the warmth and welcome of my own private, down-filled harbour. George was simply going to be there for four hours, as I was to be for another four hours in four hours' time. In a way, the sea sets too much of a test to reveal the intricacies of character. I, of course, know George ashore, the subtle and layered interactions of his strengths and weaknesses, the certainties and uncertainties, the withdrawals and generosities that make up any man. But at sea, particularly a demanding sea as it was that night, that internal play of the self does not appear. It is a simplified world and the sea only asks the simple question: are you on or are you off? Can you do this or can you not? It doesn't care why, or even how. It only expects a yes or a no.

At one in the morning, George woke me. I came up, he gave me the bearing, handed me the torch, and I took his place at the wheel. The stars were coming and going through the clouds. Our course was to leave Scilly to port and then bear away for the Irish coast. The Lizard light had sunk below the horizon but the light on the Longships reef at Land's End was still clear behind me to the east. The lightship on the Seven Stones, the rocks that sank the *Torrey Canyon*, was winking to the north of me. In the south, the arm of the Wolf ranged across the night. Ahead, Round Island light, to the north of St Martin's in Scilly, led me onwards. Beyond it, the loom of the Bishop swept out across the open expanses of the Atlantic. These names were like the constellations of the sea.

I was well that night, happy to be out here in the cold. Seasickness, as George had said to me, is a kind of fear, and like any fear can be held at bay and suppressed, can be told to get down like a dog. You can feel seasickness coming on and, as George had taught me, you can deny it. I tried it that night and although from time to time I was still being sick over the side, watching the supper I had eaten spewing out among the phosphorescence below the lee rail, it was not the sort of seasickness I had before. It didn't make me think I was about to die or my character a waste of shame. I was simply being sick every hour or so, in the way that exhaust comes out of the back of a car. Nelson was seasick until the year he died. The fear it represents doesn't need to send you to hell. And I wasn't in hell; I was in a sort of cold windy heaven.

The course for Scilly was 280 magnetic, the wind just behind the beam. One by one the quartering seas kicked under us, picking up the *Auk* first at the stern, travelling the length of her, and then dropping the bow in the trough behind. As each one came under, I held the helm against it, a door pressed shut, as George had told me, against the beast pressing in from the other side; and then, as the beast relaxed, I relaxed, taking the pressure off the wheel and waiting for the beast to try his luck again. It was a long, twice-a-minute rhythm, on and off, on and off, the wide, strong *Auk* surging into the dark.

At times like this, alone in a wide dark sea, with your companion asleep below, you can feel the wonder of a boat. Of course a boat is not a natural thing. She is the most cultural of things, the way she works dependent on a line of thought that goes back to the Bronze Age: the form of the hull and the weighted keel; the lift and drive given by a sail; the way four sails like ours can be trimmed to lead each other on; the ingenuity of blocks and tackles, strops, sheets, halyards and warps, the sheer cleverness of knots. The knowledge that is gathered in a boat is a great human inheritance, especially valuable because it is not material but intangible, a legacy made only of understanding.

You can see the boat, in other words, as our great symbol, the embodiment of what we might be. In her fineness, strength, and robustness; in the many intricate, interlocking details of her overall scheme; even in the bowing to nature of her wing-like sails and the auk- or seal-like curves of her body: in all this, she is a great act of civility. The sea is an 'it', the boat a 'she', and the courage of that confrontation is why people love the boats they know. Boats are us against it, what we can do despite the world. Each sailing hull is a precious thought, buoyant, purposeful, moving on, afloat in the sea that cares nothing for it. From the deck of a boat, out of sight of land, as Auden wrote in 'The Sea and the Mirror', his great poem on art and consciousness, 'All we are not stares back at what we are.'

There is another side to that. It is no coincidence that some of the earliest known depictions of sails, from Bronze Age Crete nearly 4,000 years ago, are exactly contemporary with the story of Icarus and Daedalus. Daedalus is the great designer of intricacies, the father of all boatwrights, the man who 'fettles' and fiddles and makes perfect an arrangement of rope and timber, who is entranced with the mimicking of nature by machine. The wings he makes for Icarus are feathered sails. When their wax fixings melt in the sun, it is a step too far, and the boy falls to his death, as the story says, in the sea. This is, at heart, not an air story but a sea story, fuelled by the recognition that the beautiful, made thing, which the winged creature of a boat represents, can fail too and bring sea-disaster on those who have trusted it. Daedalus was still in the yard at Tregatreath; I wondered, in our growing exhaustion, if we were now the Icaruses of this story.

Sometime, in the dark early hours, we came into the shelter of Scilly. I kept the boat a mile or two offshore and although the wind didn't drop, the sea went still in the islands' lee. The smell of land came wafting across the night, thick and fleshy; a warm, musty, vegetable fug, like a soup, floated out to us over the Atlantic air. I bore away on to 325 magnetic, eased the sheets, and made for Ireland. Wonderful *Auk*! Wonderful sea-surging *Auk*!

A change of watch then and again in the grey-green dawn, the grey of the sea the colour of battleships, and then again at nine or ten in the morning. On my watches, I was drifting off to sleep. George's face was creased and worn, but we were making progress. The

Auk would look after us. We were at home, however tired we were. All day, we alternated, spending half an hour or so together on deck each time, a little talk, something to eat, a cup of tea. The swells were mountainous out here, mid-passage. The whole extent of this sunlit sea was the deep, royal blue of the ocean.

On the wheel, time slid away. The sky was clear and endless, the rhythm of the boat lullingly repetitive, the sunshine bright in the eyes. Mid-afternoon, a little more than halfway across, a fulmar swung between the shrouds and the mainmast. An hour later, a swallow circled the boat, surveyed it, and without warning flew down through the companionway hatch, circling inside the cabin, cheeping, prospecting for a nest. On the way from Africa, it had found, miraculously, an almost empty, very suitable, if slightly small barn, 125 miles short of where it expected to find land. The swallow flew out again without touching timber, rope or canvas and away, its dipping, curving flight just held above the seas. Ten minutes later it returned, with another. The two of them flew down into the cabin again, not landing, cheeping in excited, quivering calls. They came out and back three more times. Surely a perfect site for a nest? Surely not: no mud or straw with which to build a home. They left again for the fourth and last time, as the *Auk* plunged on for Ireland.

If the wind had stayed good for us, we could have slid into a harbour that night as sleepily and dreamily as this day had passed. We were lulled. We could have sleepwalked home. Our exhaustion didn't matter because the *Auk* would take us on. We were her passengers.

It didn't happen like that. Late that afternoon, a weather front came through and winds veer on fronts. You could see it ranged above us, a curving wall of cloud, its leading edge quiffed up and back in wisps. The southwesterly wind that had been wafting us to Ireland shifted through thirty, forty, fifty, seventy degrees in the space of an hour. We were headed. Rain hammered down. Night was coming on again, the wind was now in the northwest, which was exactly where we wanted to go.

The bitter tide of exhaustion came flooding in. There was no way we could sail to Baltimore where we were due. The engine was the only option and the prospect of ten hours of that, at something like four or five knots, dead into a rising wind, felt like sacks of grain laid on our shoulders. The wind started to blow. For the first time now it was shrieking in the rigging. We had no instruments to measure it, but George reckoned thirty-five knots, gusting ten knots higher, Force 8 to 9. The beautiful day had given way to a raging night. We hauled the sails down and tied them as best as we could in the climbing wind. The whole of the foredeck was plunging into the breaking seas. Just visible from the cockpit, the white teeth of those breakers appeared grinning around us.

'Go down,' George said, a level of intensity in his voice I hadn't heard before. Freezing rain was driving into our faces. 'I'll get you in three hours' time.' Down below, the saloon was jumping, a savage version of itself, thrashing at the lamp that hangs from the deck-head, its chain not swinging but jerking like a hanged man, a maelstrom of no gravity followed by thumping smacking lurches into new seas. I crawled into my berth, jammed myself against its sides, my body held in place by my hands, the middle of my back and my knees, and hauled the sleeping bag up around my head. The engine groaned away beside me and I slept.

'Can you do it?' I woke to see George's masked

face slewing and sliding above me, only his exhausted eyes visible through the slit of his sodden balaclava. 'I'm too cold to stay up there,' he said. 'I'm frozen and I don't want to start making wrong decisions.'

In the churning, topsy-turvy world of the cabin, I got up, pushed seasickness away, swathed myself in the weather-armour, went on deck, got the heading for Baltimore from George, 340 magnetic now, took the torch from his hands, and he went below. I was no less exhausted than when I had gone to sleep. I had to shake my head every few seconds to keep myself awake. On and on the engine ground away beneath me. The boat was still smacking into the seas and the drench of the chilling rain was unbroken. It was just a question of staying awake and keeping us on course. No light worked in the compass. I could only find the heading with the torch. But I couldn't keep that on all the time. An occasional flash on the binnacle and then the hope for a few minutes that I was steering in the right direction. The hours stretched out ahead. The eyelids drooped closed and jerked open, again and again and again. The wool of my balaclava was wet in my mouth. The boat was being hammered by the seas we were driving straight into, coming up white on the bow and then breaking over the bowsprit. For a while the stars appeared and I could hold a constellation at least half-fixed in the shrouds, a still point in a traumatic world. But the cloud and rain closed over again. I kept looking at my watch. Ten minutes had passed, sometimes twelve. How was I going to last three hours at this? My back had tensed into steel hawsers. As I turned my head, I felt the sinews in my neck clicking and rolling over each other's armoured strands. 'Dig deep,' George had said to me as he went down.

It is a mysterious and powerful place to be, on deck alone, while the man you have been relying on sleeps beneath that deck. He has dug deep for you, has stood in his balaclava with the merest of eyeslits open to the world, shielded from it. He has stayed there for hour after hour in the dark while you have slept curled down in the bunk, protected from the rolling and breaking of the sea. How ancient a set of conditions is that? At this level, the sea is historyless: time has not passed here. His standing for me and now my standing for him is there in the Homeric poems and the sagas. It bears a cousin relationship to sharing a rope when climbing, but the tenderness of it and the demands of it are, if anything, stronger. I sleep while he suffers and I suffer while he sleeps. The only continuities are the sea, the boat, and the seemingly endless stretch of time, of an almost disconnected sense of timelessness, the repeating waves, the light head of exhaustion.

A strange and distant intimacy. The three hours came and went. I knew I must not wake him but wait until he was rested enough to get up himself. He had done the same for me, and everything here was reciprocity. It was a world governed by a mutuality of duty and care. I was cold but not impossibly cold. I was dog-tired but not beyond all consciousness. He had held the wheel for me often enough already; he had, in many ways, held me; now it was my turn.

We were in the darkest night I have known. I wonder if anyone who has not been to sea in these conditions, who has not felt himself exposed and exhausted as I was that second night, can know what it means to see the loom of a lighthouse on the shore for which you are making. It is no more than a blur at first, so faint that you cannot see it with your watching eye, but only if you look away and catch its flickering on a distant screen. Is that something? Is it? Yes, it must be. Fastnet! The Fastnet light! Again and again it smeared its paleness over the northern sky. Then another, over to the northeast, the Old Head of Kinsale. For hours they remained the two sentinels guiding me in. Lights! Land! Shore! Sleep! Home!

On the *Auk* drove, the Volvo engine beating steadily beneath me, George asleep, clearly very deeply exhausted. In the end, no more than his face appeared at the companionway steps. 'Cup of tea?' he said. The dark bulk of the land on either side was drawing us in on 340. The land now had shapes, a blacker outline against the black of the night. Ireland was a place, not a fantasy of arrival. Still an hour from the harbour entrance at Baltimore, I saw the light, marked on the chart, that I had been looking for over the previous hour. 'I've got a flashing green,' I shouted down to George. 'Make for that,' he said. The ocean slowly stilled. We reached the green, then the red beyond it, curving into the harbour calm, the lights of the village, the fishing boats against the quay, the ripple of harbour water against the *Auk*'s worn sides, the sea, as Auden once wrote, 'as calm as a clock'. We dropped the anchor at four in the morning, forty-three hours out from England, and the *Auk* lay to her chain like a stabled mare while George and I drank whisky until the sky began to show the first streaks of a green Irish dawn.

3

The Islands

We drank our Murphy's and sank into the lush of
southwest Ireland. The place oozed comfort, salmon
on every plate, scallops for every dinner. We took the
Auk in and out through the maze of islands in Roaring
Water Bay: to one side an English actor's castle, on
the other an American sculptor's island. A deep change
had occurred: there were now more ex-pat Europeans
living here than native Irish. I went to buy some fish
from the cutting shed on the quay in Schull. Eight
young aproned women stood around the steel table,
knives in hand, the bodies of the fish flipped and sliced
in front of them. They stood in total silence. I asked
the manageress, a white-skinned woman with hennaed
hair and a creased face that had once been beautiful,
why no one spoke. She was from the Loire valley,
outside Tours, and had lived here eight years. 'We do

not speak,' she said, 'because none of us can speak the same language.' Lithuanians, Estonians, Germans, Portuguese and Poles: they were all here. In Baltimore, sixteen different nationalities now lived and worked. Or so the French grocer told me. The southwestern corner of Ireland had shifted from edge to centre, filled to the brim with organic veg, face creams and lovely 'Irish' knitwear. It was scarcely the place I had left home for.

Something else lay glowing in my mind. Eight miles off the coast of Kerry, in the far southwest, were one of the beacons of my Atlantic island world. You only had to glimpse them from the mainland, or from the boat at sea, to be drawn out there. The Skelligs, a pair of tall, crocketed rocks, are strange in themselves, more upright than islands, the bigger of the two 700 feet tall but only 44 acres in extent. They hover somewhere in the middle ground – not quite islands, more than rocks. On some days, eight, ten, even twenty miles away off the Irish coast, they looked purely sculptural, as if the sea were a desk and they lay decorating it as symbols of the remote. Or when the last of the sun glazed the Atlantic yellow they seemed to be a pair of cathedrals, a black double Chartres seen from the cornfields around the city, but with their naves and chancels sunk beneath the sea, a pair of Gothic roofs. Their scale was difficult to gauge and at times, when the west wind blew, streamers of cloud tailed away from them, the summits of mountains in a distant country. These two islands are more literally attractive than any piece of land I know. They represent, somehow, a far-off centre, removed from this world but pivotal to it, a place that could not be further out – they are, with the sole exception of the Blaskets just to the north, the westernmost point of Europe – but whose isolation and history as one of the great centres of Irish monasticism a thousand years ago makes them magnetic. When the Blasket islanders went to the mainland and were thinking of returning home, they would talk of going 'back inside' to Great Blasket or Inishvickillaun. 'Inside' is what the vast exposure of the Skelligs looks like too. Their silence looks packed and pregnant.

Like many islands, grey on a distant horizon, the Skelligs invite and the boat allows, but circumstances were against us and for a week or two we couldn't get out there. Even so, as the *Auk* travelled the length of that coast, up to the Blaskets and the Arans, down past Dursey to Roaring Water Bay and Cape Clear, the Skelligs came to seem like the node of our own Atlantic geography. Skellig means 'rough place' in old Irish, a hard pair of rocks set out in the ever-swelling sea. The word in Irish for 'swell' is the same as the word for 'stomach' and that seemed from a distance to be the nature of our unvisited ambition: all crag in the soft and rolling ocean. We had to get there.

Harry Cory-Wright, a photographer from Norfolk, and Claire Cotter, an Irish archaeologist, joined the boat. Harry, who has an obsession with the Atlantic, had long wanted to photograph the ocean *from* those rocks. Claire had worked there as a summer guardian for Dúchas, the Irish state heritage service, and as a draughtswoman for the restoration project that has been underway there these last twenty years. George had been there as a young man, when skippering a sail-training vessel out of Liverpool, with eighteen world-curious Liverpudlian teenagers on board. And I was dreaming of them.

We left from the little rock and sand nook of Derrynane in a northerly, close-hauled on a starboard tack, and made a course west by northwest, out to the western horizon, where the Skelligs lay waiting. A long swell was moulding the surface of the sea. Sometimes, as we came over one of its crests, we would find a valley in front of us as long and smooth as a coombe in the Sussex Downs, sliding away before us, the slope shallowing towards the bottom, and its whole surface crinkled, as if a silk dress had been packed away too long, the fabric crazed with little ridged creases. It was an infinite set of them: the further in you looked, the more creases there were.

The hills of the Iveragh Peninsula greyed behind us. There is a glamour to distance and the Skelligs enshrine it in a way only matched, in our Atlantic islands, by St Kilda. That is why the Skelligs remain so strong a presence in my mind. Most islands you come to, from out at sea, look like a mystery, a power zone, unlike the places you have left. But all islands, when you come within that embrace, lose something of their allure. Take Scilly, for example. You cross from Cornwall, as we did on a sunny spring day, filled with high-pressure brilliance, a good eight hours from Falmouth. At the end of that day, the islands them-selves emerge from the thick air of the High like a dream country: angular, rocky places, a magical arrival, the land only visible from four miles off in smoky blue silhouettes against the sparkling sea.

When you land, you are struck by something else: the conservatism of it, the do-as-we-do orthodoxy, the net-curtain cosiness, the tight control of its resources – even commercial access to the main quays on St Mary's – by a small group of islanders. There is some strong evidence that Scilly was viewed in the Bronze and Iron Ages, perhaps by the Romans, as some kind of sacred island, even as a place for burial in the west. There is far greater density of ancient graves there, often on prominent skyline sites, than in equivalent stretches of mainland Cornwall. The ancients, in other words, may have seen Scilly as a kind of Valhalla, the great sunset destination for the dead.

In Scilly now, that edge-potency has gone, to be replaced by an almost stifling sense of upholstery and comfort, more middle than the middle, more, as one Scillonian said to me, 'like an English village than any English village I have ever been to'. Self-protective, on the make, canny enough to portray itself as sweet and forgotten, Scilly is in fact hard and mainstream. But what else, for goodness' sake, could you expect the people on Scilly to be or do? Hermits? Saints? To want an island to be a Valhalla in the west is, by definition, an idea that belongs to strangers. It is the apotheosis of 'not here'. If Scilly is your 'here', then there will be no sense of distance. I once asked a man on Barra in the Outer Hebrides what it was like to live in such a remote place. 'Remote from where?' he asked me. It is the slap in the face that every islander will, and perhaps should, give a man off a boat; which says, in effect, that you have done no more than arrive at a place where I daily negotiate the complexities of life.

But Skellig slides beyond that. It does not know about comfort. It knows only about discomfort and potency. In its intensity, its purity and its emptiness, Skellig delivers what the horizon has promised. It has been and remains, in other words, shaped from outside. It belongs to its strangers. It is the horizon drawn into three dimensions.

The *Auk* strode towards the distant rocks as though they were her natural home. George was on the wheel; Harry, with his giant mahogany box of a camera, took photographs of the sea at our feet; and Clare and I talked in the cockpit about early Irish Christianity. 'Of course,' she said in the wind, 'remoteness from the world looks like a closeness to God.'

'That is the power of distance, the glamour of

distance, the way in which an encompassed distance looks like potency.'

'It is, it is, but there's another side to it, what they call "the theology of dispossession".'

'Which is?'

'That the Kingdom is a pearl of great price, and that if you are to gain it you must give all that you have to possess it.'

'So the sea is a kind of nowhere, a divesting of everything, of every certainty, and in the nowhere, out there, is where you find the pearl?'

'A hard and rocky place besieged by the most violent environment you can imagine is the place of redemption. That's what Skellig is: a wet Golgotha!'

'The Atlantic as the setting for metaphysical drama! This is all about the aesthetics of godliness.'

'Early Christianity is quite as much a religion of the image as of the book. And look at that!' she said, pointing forward to the Gothic peaks four miles or so ahead of us. 'What does that look like to you, Adam?'

'It looks like a place full of suffering.'

'It's a place for striving, isn't it, don't you think? With a great quantity of not very much round about. It's like one of those places – in Tibet is it? – where they put the bodies out to be eaten by the eagles. It's a place for a naked meeting with things . . . It's the same for all these island monasteries on the Atlantic coast, it is a place where the *Rule* has to apply. Everything about that bit of incredibly heightened landscape demands a ferociously strict rule. It is the island of discipline. The sheer energy and subversiveness of a place like this demands it. I mean, Skellig, this tiny rock, with perhaps a dozen monks living here, became one of the most famous monasteries in Ireland, famous all over Europe for pilgrimage. And eventually that is why they shut it down in the end. There is something powerfully unregulated here, like a geyser of spiritual energy which the early monks had tapped, and when the Irish Church in the twelfth century wanted to bring this kind of local autonomy under control, the only option here was to pull them off. Pilgrimages continued – they could be centrally organised easily enough – but monks living their lives out here, that was ended about eight hundred years ago because it was too much.'

'A marine Waco.'

Claire laughed. She hadn't been here for eight years.

Little Skellig lay to the south and we altered course towards it. There is nothing little about Little Skellig. Even more than its neighbour, it is a battleship of rock, a grey, stiffened thundercloud of stone, not a blade of grass on it. But it has another colour: its ledges are white with the bodies and guano of 80,000 gannets. This is extreme unaccommodated nature. There is no compromise in such a brutally beautiful place. We turned aside to it and lay for a while under the northern cliffs as the swell surged on to them. An amphitheatre of white bodies. The gannets filled the air like snow in a glass bubble. Not a colony, not an ordained and regulated thing, but an agglomerating mass, competitive, flamboyant and difficult, a city of birds, an angry cackling above the surf, each separate from the other in precise geometrical arrangements, no gannet daring to sit within striking distance of another. A few lie dead on the lower shelves. They fish around us – the collapsing plunge into the surf, the glaucous bubbles left on its surface, a mass arrowing into the sea. It is a bird Chicago, loveless and intense. Nothing on the rock itself can sustain them. Every calorie of its life is drawn from the sea beneath us, as if the birds were an energy-pump, sucking the hidden into the visible. George blew the *Auk*'s huge and raucous hooter. The gannets paid not the slightest attention. Not a flicker. Little Skellig is a city of bird hermits, piercing, distant, far beyond us.

A mile beyond them, the sky-scraping spires of Skellig Michael were waiting. It is Little Skellig's mirror twin. The one is everything the other is not. Little Skellig is the rawest, hardest, most naked, and most impossible form of Atlantic land. No level land beyond a gannet shelf, no water, no shelter, no human presence, nothing green beyond the weed at its lower edge. Little Skellig is the world in full throb and completely unadorned. But Skellig Michael' s own naturally fearsome imagery has been taken up and transformed by the equally powerful symbolic system of the early Christian Church. Even its name enshrines that collision – the Archangel Michael comes to occupy the Skellig, the tall rough, pyramidal island, just as he had St Michael's Mount in Cornwall and Mont St Michel in Brittany.

The swell was too big that day for any of the tourist boats from Port Magee to think of landing. We would have to anchor the *Auk* on the tiny shelf of rock that extends below water for thirty or forty yards from the cliffs on the northeastern corner. The swell was coming bowling through. There was a danger that she would drag her anchor and George decided to stay with her all day. It was lucky he did. After midday, as the tide rose, the anchor started to drag and George could only hold his station by motoring on to the anchor all day. When I raised it that evening, it came up as shiny as a frying pan, polished by the rocks of the Atlantic floor.

The only place you can get on to Skellig is a little slit of an opening in which the swell rises and falls six or nine feet, and where you have to time your jump on to some steps. George took us out in the inflatable and one by one we made our leap on to the rock. George went back to the *Auk*, Harry was off with his wardrobe camera, and Claire and I entered the silence of Skellig Michael. I felt as if we had arrived at the world's navel.

Through carpets of sea campion, puffins among them, the first few hundred yards on a roadway cut by the lighthouse keepers in the nineteenth century, and then on a built stone stairway, we dived into the world of early Irish monasticism.

Skellig Michael is a severely restricted landscape.

There is no width here. It is a black hole of spiritual energy, strictly compressed, its gravity squeezed into a pimple, the ultimate in island life. The compression and restriction is what creates the symbolic landscape. Everything that doesn't matter is excluded. It is a sacred precinct, with the ocean as its boundary wall. Everything within it is made significant by that enclosure. Every microcosmic gesture here is symbolic of a macrocosmic fact. This is a nodule of holiness and suffering, of completeness and deprivation, the fulfilment of everything that is latent in the idea of an island.

Claire led me up. The beautifully restored stairs are no rustic crumbly thing. They adapt their rising to the forms of the island. They bend their way in shallow S-curves to the knobbles and protuberances of the rock. But they are made wide enough for a stream of people to climb and a stream to descend side by side. They are, in other words, a social and even an urban construction, made for large numbers of people, a crowded busy place, as it is now for those few hours when the tourist boats can get here in summer, and as it must have been on the great pilgrimage feast days of the Middle Ages. The stones are worn smooth by the feet of those who have climbed them. The long arm of the culture of Europe and the Middle East, of which this is the fingertip, reaching out into the Atlantic, has arrived here undiminished, at full strength. Skellig Michael is not St Peter's. You will find no barley-sugar gilded baldachins here; but in these steps, made only of the material the island itself has supplied, you can see the Atlantic version of those central glories.

At the saddle, the ways divide. The monumental steps continue up to the eastern peak. A rough, shaly path climbs to the west. You must choose. The establishment, the attraction of the wonderfully made thing, draws you to the east. All surprises are kept. The steps seem to climb to nowhere. They disappear over a blue horizon and of course you follow them. Christianity is not a religion of the word here, but of the involving, sculptural, enveloping image, and Skellig Michael an incarnation of an idea. In the way of all drama, Skellig springs its beautiful surprise. At the easternmost peak, just in the lee of a fin of rock that shields you from the westerlies, and on the far side of which a cliff drops six hundred feet into the Atlantic, is a miniature city. This is no cluster of rude hermits' huts. Nothing about the monastic enclosure on Skellig submits to its place. It dominates and ordains. It is the rule made stone. It brings civilisation, in the full urban meaning of that word, to the ultimate point of Europe and proclaims its overwhelming power and value there. You round the corner and are confronted by a long stone wall, fifteen feet high, without break or incident, stopping you and excluding you. It is a city wall, with a tiny doorway, through which you must stoop to pass. It looks fortress-like, a denial of the natural, exquisitely made (and restored), an act of empire. That Mycenaean wall, and the tiny entrance at its feet, has only one meaning: submit to whatever you find within.

What you find within, arranged on the lip of the precipice, with the miniature *Auk* afloat on the rolling ocean six hundred feet beneath us, is a careful piece of town planning, almost as exact as a coloured Renaissance perspective of the ideal city, arranged within a space no more than thirty yards by fifteen. It is done with precision: the tiny dark church, in the form of an upturned boat, in the centre; a *leacht*, or burial ground-cum-altar behind it, furnished with a sundial and many crumbled carved crosses as if in a cemetery (which it might perhaps have been); a paved space uniting these monuments, but also flowing around them and connecting them to a row of corbel-roofed cells slightly higher up along the western side. To the east, there are further burials beside the church, a low parapet wall, and then nothing: the 600-foot drop, pure air, and the Atlantic beyond it.

It is as tautened a space as you will ever find. On this tiny scale, a straightforward progression, a sermon in stone, develops from west to east across the precinct: from dwelling, to drinking (water cisterns tucked inside the stone walls), to prayer, to burial, to the cliff-edge, its space and the wide slow rolling of the great Atlantic waters. I looked at the *Auk* far below, her grey, stripped decks, her taking of the swells and her dipping after them, and read from her, and from my position up here, the power of smallness, of how much more this meant than any giant, gilt-encrusted church or palace could do. Skellig was a concentrate of beauty and meaning, like powder paint still in the jar, an essence long distilled.

'It's full of voices,' Claire said, 'full of silent voices.' She had been down below one evening years ago in one of the guides' huts that are on the lighthouse road, after the last of the tourists had left, and decided she might come up here to the monastery. It was a misty evening and the last of the sun was shining in spokes through the murk. Needless to say, like all islands, Skellig is a place for visions and as she climbed the long worn steps, she thought she heard something like plainchant coming down to her through the mist. As she climbed and the mist thickened, the sound grew clearer, until by the time she came to the gateway into the precinct, the voices were strong and distinct. They were in the oratory itself. Hymns were pouring out through the low doorway, the whole perfect corbelled stone box humming with the music of singing voices. She approached the opening and inside saw only the hems of black robes, bare feet and sandals. 'I thought I had died and gone to Heaven,' she said. She stood there and the singing stopped. Six Greek Orthodox monks had stayed on after the last boat had left. She left them and made her way down the long stairway listening to their chanted prayers floating down through the mist that lay in scarves around her.

This monastery is the City of God, founded on the dream of domination. It represents a wholly powerful colonisation of an utterly wild place by an utterly powerful Christian civilisation. Ed Bourke, another

Irish archaeologist who has studied Skellig Michael and for many years worked here on the Irish state restoration project, told me to remember that Christianity has a deeply ambivalent attitude to nature. 'It sees nature both as a reflection of the divine and as an embodiment of the not-divine. And that is evident here. Everything you see is clearly a response to the gob-smackingly gorgeous nature of the place. But it is also holding it at bay, and disciplining it.'

That balance and that coherence is what the early monastic tradition is about. Its aim was not madness, in the way of modern cults, but a kind of harmony. An island, particularly of this kind, distils and intensifies both what is good and what is difficult about the natural world. An island is both perfect and horrible. It is nature at its best and its worst, its most pure and its most hostile. Feelings of threat and of worship cluster here more closely than in any other form of landscape. The drive to satisfy that double impulse, in its most extreme forms, is what shaped the monastery on Skellig.

This early monastic search for understanding was in the end profoundly humane. In AD 305 the great St Antony, founder of the monastic idea, emerged after twenty years' solitude, walled up in a ruined Roman fort in the Egyptian desert. Bread had occasionally been lowered into a hole for him and groans of spiritual agony had at intervals emerged. His followers, clustered outside, waited in trepidation. What would a man look like after such travail?

Antony, as from a shrine, came forth initiated in the mysteries and filled with the Spirit of God. Then for the first time he was seen outside the fort by those who came to see him. And they, when they saw him, wondered at the sight, for he had the same habit of body as before, and was neither fat, like a man without exercise, nor lean from fasting and striving with the demons; he was just the same as they had known him before his retirement. And again his soul was free from blemish, for it was neither contracted as if by grief, nor relaxed by pleasure, nor possessed by laughter or dejection, for he was not troubled when he beheld the crowd, nor overjoyed at being saluted by so many. But he was altogether guided by reason, and abiding in a natural state.

* * *

This beautiful emergence from incarceration, so reminiscent of Nelson Mandela's slow, smiling walk from his imprisonment on Robben Island, is what, in retrospect, I imagine the quality of mind and soul of the monks on this Atlantic rock to have been. They had seen the best and the worst and had emerged whole.

It is impossible to come this far into the heart of Atlantic spirituality and not go the final step. Claire and I found Harry taking photographs at Christ's Saddle. She is frightened by heights and so would not come with us along the rough path the other way, to the western peak, the highest point of Skellig, 715 feet above the sea. In this most symbolic of places, that western peak represents Skellig's other term: not social but passionately singular, not communal but eremitic, an exercise not in domination but submission, not a denial of nature but a subjection to it, the loneliest and most entrancing place I have ever been.

After a few yards, the path is not heavily worn. Few tourists seem to go that way. It soon became obvious why. The path becomes a shaly rock-cut ledge about a foot or ten inches wide. Below, the cliff drops five hundred feet or so to the agitated sea. Above, the cliff, when you are not used to it, has a habit of pushing your body out, as if it is bulging, pregnant. Every rock is animated here. Panic comes stealing up from your boots on these ledges, a fear that rises and has to be slowly wooed and seduced into calming down and subsiding like the sea.

Then Harry and I found we had gone too far, into some ancient rock-cut cul-de-sac, perhaps a path on which the monks had picked their way to catch the fulmars that were still peering at us around every corner. Back, gingerly, to a point where a clear succession of rock-cut foot- and hand-holds stepped up the cliff for us. In none of them was the stone worn or polished like the public way up to the monastery. English stonecrop, buttons of thrift, and the long green hair of the lichen grew on their treads as well as the risers, the lines of the stone still sharp after ten, perhaps even thirteen centuries.

We climbed. All around, the world was only vertical, dropping five or six hundred feet straight below us into the incredible brightness of the western sea. The *Auk* rocked far away, as if in a cradle, in the nine-foot swell. Up here, everything stood still. A puffin turned to me at one point and the wind behind him just lifted the feathers of his cheek as if it were a hat at Ascot. A section of the stair involved squeezing crab-like up a chimney in whose walls the steps had been cut. None of it was difficult if you forgot the height. Instead, I felt, these steps, so laboriously cut, forming so intimate a connection with the distant past – they were clearly made by a man not as tall as me, the reach between them shorter than I needed – were an act of generosity. A man we could never know was showing me and Harry the way to his summit hermitage. An immense quantity of work had been done here, perhaps over generations, by one hermit after another, a restless and relentless improving of Skellig, making the physical metaphysical, making an island's holiness both explicit and accessible.

We reached a terrace that was man-made. A dry-stone retaining wall had somehow been engineered to stand up from a near-vertical rock slope and the resulting wedge of space between it and the cliff-wall filled to make a level platform about six feet wide. A small, ruined oratory was poised on its far edge. On the inner side of the artificial platform, two shallow basins had been carved from the rock where rain falling on the cliff would drain down into them. We drank the sweet water. A dead puffin lay on the grass, its breast meat eaten away by a peregrine, the pilgrim bird, whose country this also was.

On the next step above, now seven hundred feet above the sea, a further platform had been built, this time out to the west. The sun was now glorifying the western sea: golden air on a bed of golden metal. Cushions of bladder campion were growing in the entrance to another tiny ruined building. This was the highest and the westernmost point of the ancient Christian world. You could go no further. It was the end of the known solidity, the highest place, at the furthest place, encased in and enshrined by millions upon millions of acres of sunlit sea and seawashed sky.

I sat there – Harry had stayed below – and did not want to move or leave. The puffins wheeled around me. A storm petrel whirred just below. Atlantic heaven, this hermitage not gathered like the monastery in a unitary precinct, but distributed among the rock flakes of its chosen peak: an oratory here, a living space there, a garden on the other side, a water-filled rock-scoop beside it. This careful geometry is an act of discretion and intimacy, a mark of civilisation, on the most extreme point of the most extreme rock off the edge of the westernmost island that lies beyond the edge of Christendom.

The sun dropped. I went down with Harry in the twilight, as easy as going down the companionway steps, your hands behind you on the step above, and found Claire still at the Saddle. We went together to the landing, the air full of puffins on the wheel. George collected us one by one, as we jumped for the dinghy in the swell. I raised the *Auk*'s now shiny anchor, we hoisted the sails, and turned for the north. It was a night reach north to the bare shelter of Inishvickillaun in the Blaskets. The half moon glittered a broken path on the water to the west. Harry lay back in the cockpit, Claire helmed the boat in the night, making for the light on Tearacht, and I told George it had been one of the happiest days of my life. 'Why?' he said.

'I feel as if I have been let into another room.'

4

The Man

A week or two later, the *Auk* was tied up one morning next to the fishing pier at Port Magee, on the Kerry coast. I was asleep in my berth. The day was filthy, a dirty wet southwesterly, with almost zero visibility, blowing rain and fog all over us. I had poked my head out of the companionway hatch at six and decided against it. With that wind and swell, and the thick fog, there was no going anywhere. The air was filled with a penetrating damp. Back to bed, dreaming.

We had been having a high, fine time: some grey blustery days, some brilliant and glittery, the *Auk*, if I think of her now, smiling all over her face, settling into her world. One afternoon, the wind had died for a while and the sea had gone warm and still, a sudden pool of turquoise water a mile or two across. You would have seen it from a satellite, a pond of the

Caribbean carried up in the North Atlantic Drift like a drop of oil into the vinegar north. The temperature gauge on the hull registered 17.8 degrees Celsius, an extraordinary 64 degrees Fahrenheit. The wind had simply disappeared, the *Auk* had stopped and George and I both jumped off into the warmth of it. Strange moment! The *Auk* lurched here and there on the slow hint of a swell. Her sails flapped in the stillness, the spars banging as they shoved over from one side to the other and then back. From in the Atlantic I watched her moving her great bulk at sea, the underside of her belly showing grey with its anti-fouling, her topsides scuffed already from all the quays that she had gone against in Cornwall and southern Ireland, rubbed like an old clog. It is the most unsettling of experiences, to float in the sea beside your loved home like that, to watch it, and all the safety it represents, from the very element from which it is designed to protect you. You should be part of the scene you are watching; you should be there at the helm, but you are not; or coiling the ropes at the pin-rail, but you are not. You are removed into the otherworld of the sea beyond the boat. It is the nearest I have ever come to feeling like a ghost in my own life.

We had come into Port Magee the night before, just ahead of a big wind; a cold evening, with the sun dropping into the Atlantic behind us. My 15-year-old son Ben was on board, a sleepy, beautiful, long-haired presence in our own endlessly busy, what's-going-on lives. He stayed with the boat for nearly two months – his summer holidays – and, without breaking step, accepted it all, rough and smooth, dull and horrible, visionary and alarming, as though this was simply what life consisted of. I think of him now as a pool of calm in all the anxiety and excitement, a way of being that adults take fifty years to remember. He too was asleep that morning, laid out in the pilot berth, his face turned to the boards that line the hull.

Very quietly, at about nine, George woke me. 'Adam, have a look at this.' I got up and went into the cockpit. Tied alongside, attached to us fore and aft, was the most bruised and battered boat I have ever seen, at least afloat. It was a little thing, about twenty feet long, perhaps eight feet wide, its freeboard no more than eighteen inches above the water amidships: a small blue lobster boat, scuffed and scraped, the fibres of the fibreglass showing in places through the paint. A narrow, upright wheelhouse occupied the stern, big enough for a single man to stand in its shelter, a chaos of charts and papers inside, even their surfaces rubbed and worn so that they were no longer entirely legible, and a VHF radio hanging off one of the walls. In the bow was a low decked space, more like a kennel than a home, which served for a cabin. It too was a mess. Through the opening, you could see a little gas cooker in there, a thin mattress and a sleeping bag rumpled and twisted on top of it. All looked as grimy as an anchorite's cell. A lightweight fisherman's anchor was roughly tied with orange twine to a cleat on the foredeck. The lines holding this boat alongside us were frayed pieces of blue string, more abandoned washing-line than rope. Where they crossed the *Auk*'s own thick tan mooring warps, it looked like the meeting of two worlds.

This apology for a craft had arrived half an hour before, when I was asleep, towed into harbour by the Valentia lifeboat. Port Magee is a mile or two up a winding channel, sheltered from the open sea, and there is no view of the ocean from there. Nevertheless, in this wind, there could be no doubt: the sea that morning had been a mass of wild-haired greybeards.

A man appeared crouching and reversing outwards

from the grey shadows of the cabin: stained grey trousers, a light and slightly greasy brown cardigan, a big, leonine head, a worn face, the cheeks sunken and covered in grey stubble, huge, hooded eyes, his grey, sandy hair standing in a crest above his scalp. Hunched over, attempting to tidy odds and ends, he looked like an aged Rodin. Everything about him was too big for the boat, his big lanky body slack and rangy. As he looked at us, he swept his hair back from his forehead with an enormous hand.

Here was a vision of everything that shouldn't be. The man and his boat formed something the sea had chewed, tasted, shifted to the other side of its mouth and spat out: there was nothing neat here, nothing protective or protected, only a terrifyingly naked victimhood. All coherence had gone. The boat looked like a fish after a gull had picked it over. George said hello briefly to him but even though there was scarcely a yard or two between us, George and I stood there for a few moments, doing nothing but looking at him and his situation, aghast.

We came to. 'Would you like a cup of tea?' I shouted over. 'Come and warm up. Have some breakfast. You must be frozen. We've got some dry clothes.'

'Oh really?' he said, with a French accent. 'That is too kind. You Englishmen know how to be kind. It is something I know about the English. You are at heart, all of you, gentlemen.' That was the first revelation from Hervé Mahe: this uncalled-for courtesy, drawing-room speech from the half-wreck of his life.

He came on, we gave him dry clothes and boosted up the *Auk*'s heater. George made him tea and an enormous breakfast, sat him down in the saloon and, as he ate for four, we listened to his story.

He was Breton. 'I am no Frenchman,' he said when I said how much I loved France. 'I do not like the French. Nothing is more different from a Frenchman than I am. I am simply not interested in René Descartes or Voltaire or anything to do with that' – a pause for the right expression – 'French aridity.' Thirty-five years ago he had escaped the French imperialists who were taking over Brittany and had come to live in Ireland, for a kind of freedom. He was intrigued by the Breton–Irish connection and had lectured on his own culture to university students here. His accent now crossed Galway with Gallic, rolled consonants blurred into fat-bodied vowels. He was the man of the Celtic margin, a merman, an apparition from the sea.

'She's good,' he said when I asked about his boat. 'Georges, sit down,' he suddenly went on, 'I will cook you something. Do you have mushrooms? Where is a knife? Aoh, a *good* knife! Do have garlic? And oil? I need oil.' Sarah and Kathy had stocked the boat with several litre bottles of the finest Tuscan olive oil and Hervé slapped into a new one like a masseur. Soon the inside of the *Auk* was a steaming hot-tub of Hervé's mid-morning mushroom dish, a pint of double cream piling in after the bacon, mushrooms and oil. 'Do you have kidneys?' he asked, brandishing the knife like a corsair. No, sadly, no kidneys, but otherwise we had it all. Suddenly, it was life *à l'armoricaine*.

'No, no,' he said, 'she is a good one.' He had bought the little fishing boat two weeks before from a man at Kilmore Quay in the far southeast corner of Ireland. Since then, step by step, he had brought her around the coast. He was taking her to Galway, where he lived, and would probably use her to drop a few pots. He had been a fisherman before, in Brittany. He knew what he was doing on boats.

And what had happened last night? 'Ah well, last night,' he sighed, looking first at me and then at George. 'I saw you in front of me, five, six miles. You had everything up, didn't you? The main and the mizzen and both the heads'ls? Yes, a beautiful sight. I knew it was an English boat. The English know how to make a boat beautiful and I could see the grace of your boat from five miles away.' I saw Ben in his bunk, on the other side, wake up, shuffle a little and roll over, wanting to see the source of this sea-washed, Odyssean tale.

'But you got into the Sound a long time before me, when the wind still hadn't got up and the ebb wasn't running. I was trying to catch you but I must have been there two or three hours after. It was dark when I reached the mouth and the wind had picked up, and the southwesterly was running straight into that ebb, and I can tell you that is a dirty place then, a dirty filthy place. There were waves standing all the way over the sound and they were breaking. I have two pumps on the boat but one of them wasn't working and I was frightened that a sea would come on board and then it would be over. I wouldn't be able to pump it out. The boat would go down. She is a good boat but she couldn't cope with that.' I got the chart out to track his progress. Ben stared at him with eyes like mint humbugs.

'I didn't go in. I thought I might be able to find a

little place, a little corner tucked in St Finian's Bay here, where I could get some shelter from the wind. In behind there. And of course it was getting late now and you couldn't see much. I had the chart too, you know, and I was looking for this corner here, but in the end, no, there was nothing for it, I just had to anchor off the coast, here somewhere,' he said moving his hand across a wide swathe of the Irish shore.

'I put my two anchors out, at an angle like this, a V of them, and I rode out the night with them. I could not sleep, of course. The whole night we were rocking like this' – he did a dance with his hands in front of him – 'and I was praying for the morning. I was praying to the Virgin and to St Anne, the Virgin's mother. She is a saint for the Bretons, and I heard her answer my prayer. She was with me and it was her who saved me. She was with me in the night. But of course as the tide started to ebb again in the morning, the surf at the foot of the cliffs, which had been behind me all night, started to move out towards me. The waves were soon breaking just astern of me, just here, and then, with the strain of a bigger one I suppose, one of my anchor lines broke and the boat swung round right into the surf. The anchor was outside the surf but the boat was in it and I could hear the rocks in the edge of the sea grinding against each other like footballs. That is when I was down on my knees and I knew I would die. I have prayed to St Anne. I have been in a position not very different before. I did not want to die but if I die, I die. It is not the end of the world!'

Almost every one of these fluid sentences tumbling out of him down in the cabin of the *Auk* was accompanied by a sigh and a smile, a sweet ease in his face swept over at the next moment by an overwhelming anxiety and exhaustion. Again and again he stroked and squeezed his forehead with thumb and forefinger.

His little boat was rolling in the surf. The sea was on the point of taking him. His life depended on the single anchor warp. How good was it? 'It's that rope up there,' he said, 'the blue one.' He had survived thanks to the frayed blue string with which his boat was now attached to us. Had it broken, he would have been among the rocks in seconds, more likely battered to death than drowned.

At first light, a fishing boat from Port Magee, the *Ocean Star,* saw him and came to his aid. But he was so far inshore that, although they tried again and again, they could not get a line to him. The Valentia lifeboat, the *John & Margaret Doig*, had been called and eventually, after Hervé had died and been born again half a dozen times, it arrived. It was of shallower draught than the fishing boat and was able to come in close enough to get a line to Hervé and take him in tow, a hair-raising act of everyday courage by Seanie Murphy, the Valentia coxswain.

Even the way back had been hard. The lifeboat had tried to tow him around the north side of Valentia Island but it had been rough on the point and they had been forced back into the channel leading to Port Magee. There, Hervé had been taken through the steep tidal overfalls, under tow this time, from which he had turned back the night before, gripped again by the anxiety that every time a wave would come in, his one remaining pump would fail and his boat would go down. Then he was through and approaching Port Magee, and tied up by the lifeboatmen against us. They, understandably enough, had been severe and reproachful with him. What had he been thinking of, going out in a wind like that, on such a shore, with a boat so ill found?

That had been George's and my first reaction, too, seeing this piece of inhabited wreckage dragged in, as if by the scruff of its neck like a vagrant dog. But in the warmth of the *Auk* that morning, with Ben gazing down from his bunk, and the rest of us gathered round, and Hervé so passionately and honestly and forthrightly describing his night's adventures, it became impossible to see him as a victim or an incompetent. He became, somehow, more like the man we wanted to be.

Soon his conversation was ranging widely over the passions of his life. He made us all some coffee – this man who had been all night within earshot of his death – sat back in the corner of the cabin, the mugs steaming on the table in front of us, the rain hammering on the deck outside, and began to lecture me. 'Adam, listen, no, listen, you must listen,' he said his arms crossed tightly over his chest, his huge, unshaven and distinguished head drawn back like a bow to gather the energy for what he was about to say. 'What is important in the relation of man to the world is the hand.'

'The hand?'

'Yes, the hand,' and Hervé held up one of his huge hands as an exhibit, some diesel and grease smeared on it, callused at the base of the fingers, before catching hold of my wrist and holding mine up in turn. 'As long as the hand is the shaping organism of an enterprise, or a relationship, as long as it is the hand which governs your connections with the world, those connections are healthy, living and warm.' He sat back with a huge smile. A philosopher had been washed up on our shore. Ruskin was having coffee on the *Auk*.

'Technology!' he went on loudly. 'It is technology which is the great destroyer, which comes between the hand and the world, which interposes its own cold deadness between the heart and the world. Why else, Georges, are you a sailor? You are a sailor because you need to feel the reality of the world in your hand.'

George looked like he'd been given a new dad. The sterilising effects of technology were 'terrible, terrible', Hervé said. The fishing crisis would not have occurred if technology hadn't displaced the hand. The hand was the natural regulator. The hand understood when enough was enough. The early Irish and Breton saints had cast themselves on the waters, relying on no more than the sheets of their sails on windy days and the oars in a calm, both the ultimate in hand technologies. Those saints had stripped off the padding of the urban world and had *exposed* themselves to what was, to the nature of things. Truth was in nakedness like that and he quoted William Blake: ' "The body is the eternal imagination of the soul." You know that, Adam, don't you? Let us be clear about it. Let us define our positions. You must know that your body, your physical being in the world, is the full and beautiful condition which your soul has imagined for you?'

'I do,' I said.

'And which parts of the body are always naked? Where are you naked, Adam? Your face' – he held my chin – 'and your hand', which he then grasped, smiling straight at me. 'I love the English,' he said. 'When the English are like you, I love you.'

All this, somehow, seemed of a part with his near-wreck the night before. The way in which he had swept past the trauma of the night as if he were already intimate with death and was scarcely disturbed by meeting it again; his vigour, honesty, culture, commitment, his passion and his subtle, responsive mind, his frank belief, his praying to the great Breton saints, his half-broken and yet vital presence, his love of food and of this life, combined with his air of being on the margin, not like the rest of us: what was this but the soul of the Atlantic shore?

If one of those early Irish Christians, a ghost from Skellig Michael, looking for vision on a distant rock, had strolled into your life, he would surely have been like Hervé Mahe. Here, sitting with us on the *Auk*, was St Brendan himself, the man of truth, the pilgrim in the world, the stander outside the norm, a prophet of wildness and of the spiritual edge. He rolled seamlessly on to a story about one of those saints. It was clearly a set piece. Scothíne, Hervé said, was a man of great holiness and real power '*in the world*', with those words slapping his hand on the table. One day, as Scothíne was walking across the waves, he met another saint, Findbarr from Cork, who was rowing a boat.

'Why are you walking on the sea?' Findbarr asked him. Big smiles from Hervé.

'This isn't the sea,' Scothíne said. 'It's a field.' He bent down and picked a white clover flower from the water and threw it to the saint in the boat. 'And why are you rowing your boat on the field?'

Findbarr said nothing, dipped his hand into the grass, pulled out a salmon and threw it to Scothíne who caught it and held it, shining, in his hands. 'There you are,' Hervé said. 'It's the hands! The hands are the heroes of the story! Now lunch! What about lunch? What shall we make for our lunch today? Do we have wine? Do we have meat? And do we have time? Oh yes, I think we have time. Georges! Onions!'

The following morning, he left. He started up his engine, said goodbye and hoped we would meet again. We untied his lines, he began to move off, standing in his wheelhouse, heading under the bridge and up the channel towards Caherciveen. As the boat gathered way, he stepped out of the little wheelhouse and gave a big sky-wiping wave, his hand as big as a gull in the air. It was then that I saw the boat's name for the first time: *Happy Days*.

No one at Port Magee heard any more of him, but a few weeks later a letter arrived at the Valentia lifeboat house. It contained 100 euros in notes and a few lines of thanks. Hervé had brought the *Happy Days* home. 'Thank the bitter treatment of the tide,' Auden wrote in 'The Sea and the Mirror', 'For its dissolution of your pride.' Hervé Mahe, neither modest nor with any need for modesty, a man beyond pride, who had already absorbed all the lessons the tide might teach him, profoundly intimate with the realities of risk and experience, an uninsulated man, as naked to the world and its riches as any of us ever might be, had nothing to learn there. If I were in the habit of blessing people, I would have blessed him.

5

The Beach

Two weeks later, George and I had our own version of an Hervé experience. We had now embarked on making a television series about the *Auk* and her journey, and a crew from Keo Films, a London production company, had joined us. They had missed the beginning and so the boat had returned from Ireland to Padstow in north Cornwall. It was, in many ways, a beginning again, but George, I and the *Auk* were all in good shape and, from the Cornish coast, 120 miles to the south, on a good southwesterly wind, we had breezed steadily up to the coast of Pembrokeshire. It was the *Auk's* happiest point of sail, a broad reach, with the wind just coming on to her over the port quarter, across your left shoulder if you were at the helm, striking the face on the left cheek from behind, even in a gust just lifting the lobe of that ear, all sails full, their big creamy bellies curved out against the sky behind them.

All day long, coming north, the bow, as it bit into each new wave, had made that repeated wet breathy sigh, as the bulk of the new water beneath her was compressed and driven back under the hull. It's the most evocative of sea sounds, not exactly the sea breathing, nor the boat, but the steady, half-hissing rhythm of that wonderful amalgam, a boat-at-sea.

Manx shearwaters from the Pembrokeshire islands provided a kind of welcoming party for us, forty and fifty miles out from land, turning around the boat on their black scimitar wings half an inch above the wave tops, slicing through a layer of air as thin as paper above the sea. They were the real edge-dancers. If they misjudged their flight, the sea surface would trap and catch them. It never did; the shearwater is the great sea lesson: endless attentiveness and total response. I watched them for hours. All that grace is nothing but focus.

They became a symbol of everything I wanted to be and all year long George had to summon me again and again to the point. 'What's happening, Adam? And what are you doing about it? Concentrate!' The shearwater life. It became a sort of code between us. Just then, too, dolphins had come to play in our bow wave, squeaking and rolling beside us, synchronising their surges so that four or five came up together in an arc of gaiety and pure abandon, an expression of the sea at its most generous. It felt in the sunshine as if the big mother *Auk* was with her brood, as though, by some kind of miracle, she had actually given birth to them.

In that beautiful sailing expression, we soon raised the Pembrokeshire coast, our progress pulling the land up out of the horizon haze. We moored the boat overnight, away from the wind, in the harbour at Dale, a still and sheltered nick tucked in at the entrance to Milford Haven. The film crew met the boat in Dale. Not a whimper of the big swell out at sea found its way into Dale Roads, and George and I, Will Anderson the director, Ben Roy the producer, Luke Cardiff the cameraman, and Paul Paragon the soundman, all of us sat that May evening on the harbour wall outside the pub, making plans.

I had long wanted to go to Marloes Sands, a wonderful two-mile beach just around the corner from Dale, famous geologically as one of the richest in the country, with tens of millions of years of sedimentary rock layers tipped upright in the cliffs and displayed like a library of the past above the sands.

What better way of coming to Pembrokeshire than to plunge into the ancient past straight out of the breakers? We decided on it that evening. I am not sure quite why, in retrospect, none of us considered it a dangerous and difficult thing to do. Perhaps we even did acknowledge that, but slid past it in the way one does, thinking of the goal, of the good outcome, without fiddling through the details of how to get there. Plunge in and you will arrive. That was about the limit of it.

It was blowing a little harder the next morning. The crew drove to the beach, George and I cast off in the *Auk* and beat out of the entrance to Milford Haven, each tack taking us deep up against the battered red sandstone headlands of south Pembrokeshire. The seas were driving hard into them, leaving spume-stained pools of turquoise at their feet, while big modern oil tankers slid out past us, one swell after another slapping up against their bows.

By mid-morning, we had arrived half a mile or so off Marloes Sands and hove to. The swells were magnificent, whole downlands on the move. They go much faster than you think, thirty or thirty-five knots, but something about the length between crests, which can be a hundred yards or more, and their wonderfully effortless gliding ballroom motion, the sheer untroubled progress of that bulk through the sea, makes them seem slower, gentler, less powerful. Hove to there in the *Auk*, they rode up under us and past with the discretion and sleekness of a butler: fat, waistcoated, perfect. We could have sat there all day, drinking our tea, drinking up the sunshine, listening to the boom and surge, half a mile away to the northeast, of these very seas breaking on Marloes Sands.

Those breakers looked like a ruff below the cliffed neckline of the shore. Anxiety raised its little inquiring head. As George and I prepared the inflatable dinghy for me to go in, we talked about how to do it. I made sure my life jacket was tightened properly around my chest. We tied a small anchor on a very long line to the inflatable's bow fittings so that I could drop it when still outside the surf and feed myself in. That way I would have a means of pulling back out when I wanted to return to the *Auk*. The little dinghy was lurching up and down beside the yacht's hull. 'Good luck,' George said, and in the tension of it I simply passed a flat hand through the air, as if to say nothing doing, no trouble, as smooth as you like, when, of course, that was only a signal of the wild chaos by now doing a cancan in my gut. Was this really the thing to do?

Why, after all, was I doing this? Because it was a way of stepping off the safe place, an engagement with the sea, a plunging in, a way of feeling life on the skin. I knew in my heart then, and I know now, it is something no one would do who *was* properly engaged with the sea. It was a conscious dive into ignorance, into the other element. What was about to happen was bound to happen.

As I started up the outboard and took the dinghy away from the *Auk*, in towards the shore still half a mile away, George shouted, 'Just go very slowly! See what is going on, coast around the outside of the surfline and then you can judge the moment to go in. Pick it! Make sure you pick it!' I was now too tense to talk. I took the inflatable in towards the shore. I had bought it at a chandlers' in Falmouth, £1,000 of red rather handsome-looking rubber. There, at twelve foot or so, it had seemed quite a big thing. Here it was a toy, to the wrong scale as the big ridges of the Atlantic swells came strolling towards me. I watched the *Auk* herself disappear behind each sparkling ridge. The hull, the cockpit canopy, George, and the entire mizzenmast rolled below the horizon, so that for a moment only the peak of the mainsail and the top of the mainmast remained visible, a snapshot of canvas and rigging where a boat should have been, until my inflatable rolled back up to the top of my ridge and the *Auk* herself, too much of her, her whole fat body, appeared again but now below me. For a second I was looking down on to her decks, the boat exposed in plan, with George a model of a human being in the cockpit.

It was a slow-motion roller coaster, but I was all right with it, constantly shifting my weight in the dinghy to counteract the rise and fall of the sea, up on to the side sponsons as the swell lifted beneath me, down on to the floor of the boat as they went through and past. I was taking the dinghy back and forth just outside the surf zone, watching the sets roll into the sands, getting used to their pattern, three big ones and then a pause, a passage of lower swells, three more and then a pause. The engine was responsive in my hand. I would wait for the last of three and then go in hard for the shore.

It didn't happen like that. Looking landward, I felt the familiar rise behind me of the next big one coming in. I shifted, still without looking, to the seaward side of the dinghy, to take my weight over there as the swell came through. But then – simply through the geometry of my body and the boat, by the steep angle at which the boat and I were now tipped – I knew that this one was different.

I looked behind me. Out to sea, still seventy or eighty yards away, with its crest breaking and the sunlight burning through the bright thin fin of water just below it, I saw the biggest wave I have ever seen coming towards me. It was steepening with every second; the impossibly white crest was lengthening and deepening as I watched. It was perfectly clear, even in that first second, that the whole thing, the whole green, heavy, and increasingly lowering wall of water was going to dump itself on top of me, fill the boat and maybe – this was my thought at the time – drive me back out of the boat like a knife scraping food off a plate. The sheer size meant that it was breaking far outside the surf zone of all the others. I was already in its surf zone, just at the most dangerous point, the biggest wave I have ever seen coming to get me.

I know now what I should have done, or at least tried to do. I should have turned the boat shorewards at that moment and ridden with it, going with the engine at full throttle, taking me inshore on a big boiling mass of surf, a chaotic sleigh ride into the beach.

But I didn't. I didn't have the gumption. At the time I thought my only option was to turn into it and take it on the bow. I had only just made that decision when I realised it was the wrong one, but too late to do anything about it. I certainly couldn't turn sideways on now. The boat began to climb the vertical face of the wave, I leant forward because I thought the wave was going to break over my head and I didn't want to be washed out of the back. But the wave didn't break over the boat; it simply turned the boat over, bow over stern, a slam-dunk, head-over-heels, throwing me out as it did so.

It goes slow then. I am underwater and under the boat. The wave is breaking through me and over me, an aerated chaos of half-lit green. I am no way up but I am under. I didn't know it at the time, but the anchor that George and I had put in the bow fell out as the dinghy went over. It hit me in the face, cutting my forehead, cheek, and upper lip. All I knew was that my face felt hit, as if punched, sore in the salt water. And then I was up in the light and the air, breathing, looking at the sky and its bobbled clouds. No sooner had I emerged, than another of the big ones, the big seas, the sea monsters that can consume you more easily than any sea monster with fins and tails ever could, was on me again and I was rolling down into its turn and overturn. Back up and breathing, the dinghy beside me now upside down, with the shaft of the outboard sticking up above it and the propeller still turning in the air, the two of us, the boat and I, slurping in the big valley between two swells. Another coming. My life jacket. Why hadn't I inflated that? How to inflate it? I thought it was one of those self-inflaters. No, as flat as when I had put it on. Pull the toggle. Where was the toggle? I was scrabbling for it, unable to see it or feel it or find it with my fingers, as the third of the huge breaking seas came through me again and that, for a few seconds, is when I thought I might drown.

Down deeper this time into the roll of the surf, suddenly alarmed at the idea of the dinghy itself, and its protruding outboard, coming slamming on to my head as I was down there, and the feeling of enclosure, of wanting to shout, but the water of course clogging me into silence, a wet muddled claustrophobia like the worst of a bad dream, a fear like a nightsheet twisted around your head, into your mouth and nostrils and neck, a gag on your life, a garrotting by water.

This was the sea in its killing horror, the death element, the antithesis of life. This moment, seen face to face, was the reason that people have always, from the very beginning, loathed the sea. The *Odyssey*, which is not only the first but the greatest sea poem ever written, as old as the tumuli in which chieftains lie buried on the hills of southern England, and older than the great hillforts that straddle the skyline beside them, is suffused not with love of the sea but fear of it. Odysseus – the first great middle-aged hero in literature; his poem the story of the Middle-aged Man and the Sea – longs to go home, to the sweetness of land and the stillness of a house. But the loathing of Poseidon, the sea god, encloses him in one near fatal sea-trap after another. That is one of the *Odyssey*'s central meanings: the sea itself is the element of death. And nowhere more powerfully than in the land of the dead, which Odysseus finds at the very limits of the known world. He travels there only so that Tiresias, the blind seer, can tell him how he might return home.

> The sail stretched taut as she cut the sea all day
> and the sun sank and the ways of the world grew
> dark.

These are the outer limits, the edge of the Ocean River, a desolate coast, where the only trees that grow are 'tall black poplars and willows whose fruit dies young'. The waves break on a darkened beach. Hell has never seemed so beautiful.

I came bursting to the surface. As I rose, not knowing if I was rising or falling, I was looking with my fingers for the toggle on the life jacket, scrabbling in its folds with my fingertips, like a piglet or a lamb desperate for the nipple, some source of life. At last I found its little plastic berry, stuffed in between the Velcro it should have been hanging below, pulled it, triggered the canister of CO_2 and *wwoohoosh* – up came the wonderful life-giving life jacket around me like a meadow, a home, a bed, a pillow, a nurse, a life. I laughed aloud alone in the sea! Never have I felt so happy. My life jacket held me. I was safe in its arms. I was somehow free of anything the sea could do to me, more free than I could ever have been on land. Life in the arms of death. Escape from Hades.

What was this? Some adrenaline high? I don't know, but I lay there ecstatic in my new buoyant state. The propeller of the outboard had stopped turning. I had to decide what to do. I thought at first I would swim to the shore, as if nothing had happened, and go on to look at the geology of Marloes as planned. The film crew I knew were on the beach. I could stroll out of the surf like Odysseus and start looking at the rocks. What else could this new-given life be for? And so, doing backstroke and my arms windmilling, I started heading inshore. The inflatable, upside down, stayed where it was because the anchor was now holding it in place. Occasionally, a big sea like the one that had overturned me came thundering through, but that was fine. My mother and father of a life jacket held me up on the surface. However broken the sea, I floated.

I was making progress shorewards when I heard George shouting. George! I had forgotten about him. He was something from the time before! Suddenly, extraordinarily nearby, but cut off by the body of a swell between us, I saw the very top of the *Auk*'s mainmast, a strangely unreal sight, just the radio aerials and the whirling cups of the anemometer, the rest erased by the bulk of the sea. It was about a hundred yards away. George had come to save me, bringing the big ocean-going *Auk* deep into the surf zone! The charted depth of the place he had come to get me was about eight feet. The *Auk* draws six. There was a real possibility that the swells could have dumped the boat, in one of their troughs, straight on to the bottom. God knows what would have happened; perhaps the hull fatally strained, the succeeding crest simply breaking all over it, overwhelming the cockpit and pouring below, sinking the *Auk* there and then, breaking it up, churning it into a vast quantity of smashed lumber awash beside me, with George in it, the most dangerous situation conceivable: a tumbling sea filled with jagged and hard-edged spars, the shards of hull and deck, a mobile bed of knives.

George could see nothing of me. I couldn't see him, but I could see the *Auk*, the place of safety, which in trying to rescue me was endangering herself and him. I could hear him shouting: 'Adam, Adam, come to the boat. Come to the boat. Come to the boat.' He didn't know I could hear him. He was shouting at an empty sea still breaking in its slickbacked ridges along the whole length of Marloes Sands. All he could see was the upturned dinghy, with the shaft of its outboard still vertical like a flag of futility.

Then I rose on one of my crests, and there he was, looking back at me from the cockpit, but sailing away now, the boat in the wind powering away, heeled over, her wake full and white. I held my two hands in the air, thumbs up – not the right signal, I know, because two hands up are a conventional sign of distress at sea – but George made the same sign to me in return. We were together, neither of us broken, both alive, communicating, all right.

I flailed out towards the deeper water. He tacked, came back to me, hove to, and suddenly the *Auk* was there beside me. Huge bodies of swell and surf were still sweeping past us on the very edge of the breaking zone. It was not the place for a big-displacement yacht. Every fifteen seconds or so, twenty-two tons of boat were rolling hugely towards me and then away. One minute I was nearly level with the deck, the next seeing the huge grey underbody of the thing exposed like the flank of a whale above me and over me, not a haven but a hammer. George had the webbing ladder down over the side. I needed to get my feet on the bottom rung just as she rolled towards me, and then have myself lifted up by the roll of the boat itself. At the same time, George had to lean down and get me by the back of the life jacket. There is a lifting hoist there for helicopter rescues. We struggled with it, George saying, 'Come on, come on, get on, there's no time here.' At about the third roll I got it right, the *Auk* hauled me from the sea and I turned myself over on to the side-deck like a walrus, an exhilarated walrus, saved from the deep, a spreading smile all over my face, happiness cascading through me. George was looking anxiously into my face, to see what damage was there. There was none, only a surf-delight in the cataract of wet chaos in which I had been riding for half an hour. He looked the burdened man. Will Anderson, the Keo Films director, was on the VHF from the beach, wild anxiety in his voice. '*Auk*, *Auk*, *Auk*. George. Is he all right? Is he all right? How is he? Have you got him on? Is he OK?'

'Keo, *Auk*,' George said, the flattened voice of the man long at sea. 'He is absolutely fine. More than fine. I've never seen him better. Wet but fine.'

If I'd ever needed a lesson that the tension and anxiety around death is not experienced by the dying, but by those who are forced to watch, this was it. I had never felt so free. Will sounded and George looked exhausted with the worry. I felt as buoyant as a balloon.

The inflatable remained anchored upside down in the surf. The only way to get it was by land, and so we sailed back into Dale and met the film crew there. Every one of them stared interrogatively into our faces. I babbled like a maniac on speed.

They took us in their bus round to the beach. There was the little red boat riding out in the surf, three or four hundred yards away, bobbing like a duck, but a drowned duck, upside down, the outboard immersed. The surf looked impossible from here, a field of broken water stretching away from us a third of a mile, grey with the sand in it, towering above the beach, one ridge after another driving on to the shore. How could I ever have thought I would cruise in through that? Feckless arrogance subjected to the acid of the sea. No landscape can be as moral as this.

George was worried that, as the tide withdrew, the boat would be beaten to shreds against the sand in the shallows. He is a powerful swimmer, who has rescued people before now. He said, 'Come on now, let's do this, I want you with me', and so we plunged in together. I tried but failed to make any headway against the surf that was beating into us, the walls of water knocking me back. Will, who was standing on the beach, waded in up to his knees and shouted, 'Adam, Adam, come back. Come back. You can't. Don't, just don't.'

But George was swimming out there, backstroke, through it all. Heaven knows how he did it, beating out through the surf, appearing and disappearing within the ridges of the swell, like an ant crossing a ploughed field. Ben Roy stood on a rock to one side and directed him first one way then another, sema-phoring with his arms, which George apparently from time to time could see.

Finally, he reached the boat and climbed on to it, attached a line to one side, stood on the other, and with his weight tipped the thing over. It is what I should have done in the first place. He pulled the anchor up, lay flat in the bow of the boat, and with his arms began to windmill the boat ashore.

We watched the rescue. The crisis was over. A conclusion had been reached. But then I saw – we all saw, the whole crew watching on the beach saw – an enormous wave, far bigger than the others, coming up behind him, steepening above him, climbing to heights where it could no longer remain a wave. It was pushing up the stern of the inflatable, the breaking at the crest spreading and deepening as we watched, and then in a rush and chaos of white water the inflatable was tumbled over. What had happened to me was happening to him.

After it had gone through, the inflatable was there, still the right way up, but George had disappeared. We looked at the grey surf, the succession of smooth-skinned swells beyond it and the empty red boat slowly being pushed in by the wind towards the shore. No sign of a man, no small black dot of a head, or the ant-like motions of a clambering body. He must have been thrown out by the big sea, perhaps sent down as I had been into the tumbled chaos of the broken water. But it was shallower here. Had he been thrown against a rock, knocked out, drowned and gone? Was he gone? Was George gone? The inflatable was moving steadily on towards us. Death and absence had strolled on to the scene. He had been wearing no life jacket. Why not? Because he wasn't. And now his body was out there somewhere, floating, or pinned and caught. All we were left with was the heartlessness and nothing there.

In one of Wordsworth's rich, image-potent dreams, in Book 5 of *The Prelude*, he meets a Bedouin in the desert, but the Bedouin on his camel will not wait for him and rides on – he is always looking back behind, with fear in his eyes and 'his countenance disturbed'. In his dream, Wordsworth joins the Bedouin, looks back too and sees:

> A glittering light, and ask'd him whence it came.
> 'It is', said he, 'the waters of the deep
> Gathering upon us . . .'
> . . . I call'd after him aloud;
> He heeded not and before me full in view
> I saw him riding o'er the Desert Sands,
> With the fleet waters of the drowning world
> In chase of him, whereat I wak'd in terror . . .

The condition of the sea is murderous. Homer calls it 'wine-dark' not because that is its colour, even in the Aegean, but because that is its nature. It is thick with the intoxication of darkness. It is loved, sentimentally, by the ignorant and by romantics because death is the moment for which Romanticism longs, and because, as Homer knew, and as my own panicked crisis now told me, no moment is more vivid than one embraced by death.

That is why death at sea is such a casual affair. Death has no need to approach. It doesn't need to gird itself up here. It doesn't come rolling on like a swell, proceeding grandly towards you with its bosom before it and its intentions clear. Death is already there, a few feet away, resting beneath the table, its head on its paws and a smile in its eyes, happy to accept the scraps that fall.

Bleakness on the beach that morning on Marloes Sands. 'Can you see him?' I said to Will. 'Can you see him, Paul? Ben? Luke, can you see him?' They all shook their heads at me in silence, preserving their roles, even now, behind the camera, maintaining their non-presence even as I was interrogating them, the fiction that I was the only person there. I stared at the sea and at the beach. Ben Roy, doing his job, the camera still rolling, the boom-mike held by Paul above me, said, 'How do you feel?'

'How do I feel? How do I feel?' I said. 'How do you think I fucking feel?' Luke put down his camera and Paul brought down his boom, collapsed its telescopic lengths and turned the tape machine off. We stood there looking at the sand, as the stupid boat came rolling in, with the endless waves around it. Will got on the phone to the coastguard and the lifeboat. A helicopter was called. A boat was coming.

How did I feel? Not, as one might imagine, shrieking with horror, but stunned, broken, killed off, feeling as though something had happened outside the normal run of things. As if George dying in front of us was not earthly, not part of how things were. George was dead; George was dead; but everything was the same; George was dead; everything was odd; everything was not right. Where in God's name was he? Where was his head that should be visible in the sea? Was that his head? Could they see his head? Where was George? Where in Jesus's name was the man who had gone to get the boat? Where for Christ's sake was he?

How honest can I be? There are also ignoble thoughts at moments like this. Later, I asked Will what his had been. 'I was wondering what the terms of the company's insurance policy were like.' At the same time I was thinking, mixed in with the gut-hollow of George being dead in the sea in front of us, 'I wonder how I can take the *Auk* on without him? What is going to happen to this voyage of ours?' How, in other words, will this affect me, my wellbeing and my plans? It is a sobering recognition: if there is one thing more ruthless than the sea, it is the self-serving instinct for survival.

George was not dead. He was in the surf, behind the boat, hidden from us by the boat, holding on to it and acting as a drogue in the water, trying to stop it being driven too fast ashore. Within ten minutes of his reappearance he and the inflatable were on the beach. George was full of smiles. And what was our reaction? Not welcome, nor relief, nor comfort for the man who had been *in extremis*, who had done a brave and capable thing, but anger. I welcomed George, but I didn't feel like welcoming him. I told him how devastatingly difficult those four or five minutes had been. He said, 'Come on, come on. Don't fuss. I was always fine. Really.' All I could think to say was that it hadn't been fine on the shore.

George in the sea, and those of us on the beach,

had experienced different events. He was now way up on the excitement. I, anyway, felt that somehow I had been wrongly exposed to grief, that I had been made suddenly vulnerable when I shouldn't have been; that the killing nature of the sea had entered me more deeply in those few minutes than ever before, and certainly far deeper than in my wet adventure of the morning, but on false grounds. I felt angry, I realized, not with George, but with the situation, the facts, perhaps with the sea itself.

Ben said, 'Let's go and get drunk', which we did. All of us. And that night, rocked deep in my bunk in the *Auk*, I remembered something read long ago: the first thing which the author of the Book of Revelation noticed in his vision of the end of time. The most beautiful aspect of the new heaven and the new earth that had been revealed to him was this: 'there was no more sea'.

6

The Edge

I am 45, too old to be sent to war. I am Odysseus's
age, and Nelson's during the long blockading cam-
paign that led to Trafalgar. I should have had my war,
but, in common with the rest of my generation, I have
avoided it. I have lived my life in a pocket of safety,
four and a half decades of deciding where to go on
holiday and what car to buy, what book to write, what
film to see, what journey to embark on. It has been,
in other words, a period in which any kind of courage
has not been required. Our belts are loose in a way
they haven't been since – when? Regency England?
The Restoration? Our fears are the very opposite of
those that have stalked people in the past. We are
anxious that life is not dangerous enough; that it bores;
that it's stale; that it lacks 'dynamism'. We are terrified
our existence might be inert or dead.

That was the reason I was here. This oceanic threshold was the source of vitality, strangeness, and gripping seriousness that the ordinary life, the life without challenge, or only the boring, deadening form of challenge normality provides, could never have given me. It stood in for my generation's missing war.

But this is a subtle and layered area. In many ways, perhaps as far back as the *Odyssey*, the sea has played the role in the western imagination of the dynamic and lyrical margin, the place whose danger is revelatory, and whose challenge summons the deeper virtues. And, particularly for the English, it is the western sea that does that. The east and south are prose; the west and north the poetic and the exposed. The west is like a descant to the land and its sea surge runs through the veins and arteries of the English imagination. In *The Enchafèd Flood*, W. H. Auden's series of linked essays on the part played by the sea in the European imagination, he quotes one of Edward Lear's limericks:

There was an Old Man of Whitehaven,
    Who danced a quadrille with a Raven;
    But they said – 'It's absurd, to encourage this bird!'
So they smashed that Old Man of Whitehaven.

The desire for the sea sets itself against everything that is represented by Edward Lear's 'They'. The angry, smashing, strangeness-destroying They; the dinner-party They; the decayed, normalising, tight, dreary, hypocritical They: all of that is simply absent out here on the Atlantic waters.

If you hope the world is alive, then you should cast off and open the oceanic door. The chart is what matters. On its eastern side, the land with its exactness and its definitions. On the left, the great waters, the realm of openness. 'If man remains without possibilities,' wrote Kierkegaard, also quoted by Auden, 'it's as if he lacked air.' Air and possibilities are what this eternally open, western margin has by the bucketload. In reducing you to a sick, stormbound or storm-tossed bit of flotsam, or allowing the threads of self-reliance to develop in you, or the seeds of grit to harden in your gut, the ocean threshold gives you your freedom. As the Scottish writer Alasdair Maclean wrote in *Night Falls on Ardnamurchan*, the beautiful and bleak elegy to the end of a form of Scottish west-coast consciousness, 'The physically deprived are the spiritually deprived.' It is in some ways just a question of room, of expanse, of a felt largeness to life.

But there is something wrong with this. Remoteness, or out-of-touchness, is nowadays a choice rather than a condition. What feels, in one sense, like the deepest of engagements with the real world, the actual physical circumstances on a rocky and at times difficult shore, is in another way the most unreal situation you could imagine, a pretend reality, floating on the huge balloon of cash it takes to get a yacht to sea, disconnected from the serious, adult things that matter – politics, geofinance, the realities of getting on in the real world.

Maybe our holiday-tasting of this other reality is just an exercise in self-delusion. We can put up with the discomforts of an earlier, very physical existence only for a while before returning to the comforts our real lives provide. There is a salutary remark for all holiday fantasists made by the guru Georges Gurdjieff, the early twentieth-century prophet and teacher who began life as a Greek in the Russian Caucasus and ended it, admired if only half understood, in Paris. The story is set a little earlier in Manhattan. Gurdjieff, speaking English, but his accent as thick as the pelt of an Abkhazian bear and his manner both obscure and broken, was meeting some disciples in a Lower East Side café. One was a rich young man who had decided to give it all up, to leave the city and everything the city represented, to abandon all that for a life far away, out in the out-of-touch world where, Thoreau-like, he would bury himself in the deep leaf litter of a natural existence. 'So, Mr Gurdjieff,' he asked at the end of his speech, 'do you think that sounds like a good idea? Do you think that's the way to go?'

Gurdjieff, master of the pause, a miraculous air of authority hanging about him, delayed and delayed before making his deep and grumblingly important reply. 'It is a good life,' he said in his beard, pausing again while the American waited for his destiny to be steered and settled by the man he admired more than any other. 'Yes, it is a good life,' Gurdjieff repeated, 'for a dog.'

Of course he was right. There *is* something incomplete and slightly doggy about those who have gone to live in deep out-of-touch country, abandoning the urban as too unsettling and too unpredictable. Those dogs who have chosen to live in the furthest flung corners of the world seem slightly reduced by it. It is as if, away from urban pressures, they have gone slack. Their whole existence tends to become jowly, like a sail whose sheets have been loosened. They do not appear liberated or energised by their decision, but made dull by it. We've all glimpsed them in off-season Cornish or West Cork bars or, later in the year, with a tan so deep they look as though they have been cured in brine for a couple of months and now have no energy left for anything but reaching for the next cigarette and applying the lighter flame to its tip without the elbow even leaving the surface of the table. They've given up talking; they've given up the social disciplines that cities represent without really adopting the mores of the places they have adopted. All they can do is growl, wag, and whimper when there is the prospect of food or drink in the air. It is surely no way to go.

My year, as you will have gathered, has been spent exploring these confusions. I understand what Gurdjieff meant, but I don't believe that the Gurdjieff slump is the inevitable outcome. I don't see why choosing to live in a more exposed way than the usual should leave one collapsed and effete, the victim of your own self-indulgences. There is surely a more positive outcome than this?

As the broad arms of the lovely *Auk*, a washerwoman, a mum, took us north to the wild places, we realized, if we got things right, that I could spend the weekend on the great annual pilgrimage to the top of Croagh Patrick, the scree-covered mountain that stands over 2,500 feet high in the far west of County Mayo, overlooking the islands and channels of Clew Bay. The mountain, on the very borders of the Atlantic, is known locally as the Reek – it looks from a distance like one of the old rounded handmade hayricks one still occasionally sees in the small fields of the west of Ireland – and every year, on the last Sunday in July, a mass of pilgrims toils its way up the rough and stony path to the church on the summit.

There were said to be 60,000 people there that Sunday, and from the little village of Murrisk at the foot of the climb you could see the multicoloured ribbon of them, a three-mile-long piece of bunting, flickering slightly with its own movement, laid out across the long grey stony slopes. The uppermost stretches of the column reached up and disappeared into the mist that clothed the summit, the colours of their clothes absorbed into the grey of the cloud. It was like an image of people ascending to Heaven.

Even that sight, from a distance, was extraordinarily moving: a river of humanity, all ages – grandmothers, four- and five-year-olds; an old man wearing what was clearly his best suit putting one dogged foot in front of another, grindingly slow, holding a thick ashplant and wearing a dairyman's rubber glove on his hand to protect it from chafing; athletic young men beside him, others clearly past their best, sweating and groaning with the rigours of the climb. At times, particularly when we were enveloped by the mist and rain, and as those descending struggled past those still on their way up, slithering on the loose stones, often haggard with the effort, it felt like a scene from a film of refugee peoples, or a Dantean epic of heaven or hell, vast crowds straining past each other, a broken half-murmur of conversation and encouragement between them, most in silence or near-silence, but some small parties constantly 'yapping and gobbing', as one pious woman described it to me. 'But one must not judge. Even if they are yapping and gobbing, they may still be with the Lord. No, no, one must not judge.'

A very small minority, perhaps one in five hundred or so, were doing the climb without shoes or socks and I joined them barefooted myself. The pilgrimage is said to have been in continuous existence for almost 1,600 years, ever since St Patrick spent forty days and forty nights on the mountain, tempted by the devil and then making a series of bargains with God by which the Irish would be granted special dispensations at the Day of Doom.

Doing the climb in bare feet could be seen as a form of repentance for past sins: one woman I met was suffering the tortures of the shoeless climb not because of anything she felt she might have done herself, but for 'the sins of the dear departed'. It was her dead husband, she explained, whose wickedness needed accounting for. Another man I walked with, Michael John King, a charming, witty, and deeply religious mountain guide from Clifden, further south on the Atlantic coast, said he had taken his shoes and socks off and exposed his feet to the often needle-sharp rocks of the mountain simply as a kind of thanksgiving for the good things which life had brought him, and for being saved from any accidents in the year that had passed. Another man said he was doing it for world peace. Another because a child of his was afflicted with asthma. And yet another saw it, he said, simply as a means of getting in touch with the nature of the mountain and the meaning of the pilgrimage itself.

That, in some ways the most obscure, was the version that made most sense to me. Gaston Bachelard, the French philosopher and writer on the poetics of space, famously wrote: 'You cannot remember time; you can only remember the places in which time occurs.' That is the understanding that lies behind all journeys, especially pilgrimage, and particularly a six-hour, increasingly painful pilgrimage up a sharp-edged mountain on the edge of the Atlantic. The pain in the bottom of your feet – 'God have mercy on your soles' one man said to me with a toss of the head as he strolled past in his pair of £150 rubber-cushioned mountain boots – and more particularly, perhaps, the ever more delicate care with which you set your feet down on the mountain, picking out the smallest patch of smooth stone in the field of razor-spiked pebbles, is the most effective mnemonic I know. It makes the landscape into a memory machine, so that now, months later in the winter, long after my soles have ceased to burn, I can remember almost literally every step of the way.

But how, you will ask, as I did, can that connect with any aspect of religion? How can pain in the feet have anything to do with a child who has asthma, or a dead husband's indiscretions, or a relationship to

God? The answer is perhaps largely to do with humility. 'That is a mountain,' Ernie Sweeney, one of the great talkers of Castlebar, not far from the foot of the mountain, had told me the day before, 'which glorifies the humble and humbles the glorified.' More than that, it attempts to use the landscape as a theatre for the relationship between God and man. Hard pilgrimage recognises that the instinct that drove Christ and Patrick and the thousands of other Irish saints into the wilderness is not a historical phenomenon but a religious metaphor that can be perfectly vital now. The barefooted walk up Croagh Patrick, as I thought of it anyway, is an abandoning of comfort for a while as a means of understanding what the world is like. Exposure to the rocks is exposure to the nature of things, and your own hopelessness in relationship to them. Pain shows you how things are. I told Ernie Sweenie, when I came down the mountain, that the pain made me feel like lying down and dying. 'Well, if you did,' he said, 'you'd go straight to heaven like a rocket. There'd be a hole in the ozone layer to show the way you went.'

7

The Crew

As the summer wore on, and as we made our way north up the Irish coast and then crossed over to the southern Hebrides, something seemed to go wrong between George and me. It was distressing then and it is distressing to write about it now; but whatever went wrong between us is, I think, connected with the nature of a journey like this. The Atlantic shore, and the experience of it in a small boat, makes relentless demands on people and is unforgiving in its exposure of them. Every man emerges naked from the sea and I think, in some ways, what went wrong between George and me was the result of that exposure. It took a long time for that to become clear and the extraordinary climax and resolution of this difficulty didn't finally come until we were in Orkney. When it did, I could scarcely have been more surprised.

We had already been through a great deal together. The first long crossing to Ireland; meeting Hervé and absorbing his example; the incident on the Pembrokeshire coast; our long talks together about the relationship between boat and home, sea and shore, us out here, Sarah and Kathy back in England. Insulating layers had been stripped away and in some ways now the wires lay bare between us.

The day on Skellig, for me like ten hours spent in a glowing crucible, had been followed by a bad night in the Blaskets. George had been unable to leave the *Auk* at the Skelligs. All day he had put up with the difficult combination of anxiety and tedium, sitting alone on the boat, wondering if its anchor was going to hold, knowing that the rest of us were on the island drinking in its every element, while he could only watch from the side. Demand without stimulus, accommodating the necessary and ever-present watchfulness, needing to check at every turn that the boat was continuing to cling to its tiny underwater shelf with its toothpick of an anchor, ten or twelve fathoms below. He was, as a result, exhausted, even before we arrived late, at one in the morning, at the frankly unsatisfactory shelter we had chosen.

The anchorage in the lee of Inishvickillaun had scarcely been sheltered from the westerlies and the swell had poured through the gap to the north of the island. The *Auk* had been unsettled all night. None of us had tightened the mizzen sheet, and so its jaws were twisting and grinding against the mast all night. In the broken water that came round the top end of the island, halyards and their blocks were slapping against the mainmast. The anchor chain was continually grinding against its fairlead in the bow, a low rumbling.

All night long, George was up and down, more aware than the rest of us of the possibility that the anchor might not hold. He was clearly angry. On one occasion as he went past my bunk to the companionway steps, the boat tipped so severely that the kettle fell off the cooker and veered all over the floor. I lay where I was and said, 'Can I do anything to help?'

'That's what's called a BSR,' he said.

'A BSR?'

'A Bum Slightly Raised.' And none of you need bother with the fucking kettle.'

Then, sharply, and at other times more subtly, my hopelessness and lack of responsibility was twinned with his anger. It became something of an underlying theme. George of course knew a great deal more about the psychology of the sea than I did. He had watched it at work on people, including himself, for too long not to be familiar with the dynamics of crews and with the way that adequacies and inadequacies overlapped at sea. He had often talked about the way the sea draws people who do not feel entirely whole on land. Even my presence here this year was a symptom of the belief that a boat could solve your problems. A boat, for all its complexity, is in fact a version of simplicity, but of a satisfyingly complex kind. Get to know the hundreds of ways in which a boat-at-sea works and you become its master and commander. A boat provides control in what looks like uncontrollable circumstances. It is the mirror image of the realities of life on land, which look easier but are, psychologically, far more difficult, more subtle, less visible, and less predictable. The boat, in other words, is the haven from the storms at home. And because a boat's workings are a mystery, in the old sense that it is an arcane art, with its own equipment and vocabulary, its nostrums and obscurities from which the vulgar are excluded, it is also a source of potency and seduction.

George had known glamorous yacht skippers in the Caribbean. As he saw, there was always something hollow about their potency because everyone at sea, in one way or another, had run away to sea. The cool of a cool yacht skipper belonged more to the yacht than the skipper. Divorced from his craft, in all its senses, the sailor becomes a diminished man, his prop not there for his elbow to lean on.

George knew all these things but was at times subject to them too. There can be few people in the world as capable as him: a natural athlete, a charming and funny man, an incomparable mimic, a gifted musician, a man who sticks to tasks and knows how to dig deep, who will go ten miles before you have asked him to go one. But alongside all that, his need to exert control over the boat and its inhabitants, particularly when tired, could be powerful. He would ask me, say, to lash a dinghy to the deck, come back when I had done it and kick it to show I had done it wrongly or badly. He would ask me to attach a line to a mooring buoy or a quayside without showing me how, and allow me to struggle before showing me the right way. Rarely would he accept that anything I had done was done right. Some of my children had left their beach buckets and spades on the boat: they became somehow symbolic of my messiness and unsuitability to boat life, or my 'guilt', as he said one day, about leaving the children behind. In part, I felt, what mattered to him most was the boat, as a destination in itself, when what mattered to me was what the boat might do and where it might go. An air of frustration hung about him.

I don't wonder, because what I had asked him to do for me was not easy. It is a version of the old predicament for a boat owner and the skipper he employs. The boat owner knows what he wants to do and the skipper knows how to do it. Even if that relationship has a dose of resentment and difficulty built into it, it is straightforward enough compared with our situation. With George, not only was I his employer, but also his crew. I would tell him what I – and, even more, the director of the TV programme – would like to do and he would then tell me to do it. The poor man had to look both ways, listening to and instructing the same person. No wonder he felt taut.

This difficulty was made worse by my own lackadaisical, freedom-searching, and non-mechanical frame of mind. The qualities I love in my son Ben – a kind of disengaged ease about things – George found wildly frustrating in me. He dreamed, he often told me, of the two of us becoming such a good crew together that there would be no need to talk. The boat would simply happen. It would go on its way as sleekly and neatly as an Atlantic panther.

In his eyes anyway, that never occurred. Although he did once say that maybe it was because he was refusing to let me grow out from under his shadow, George never felt that I could skipper the boat myself. I did! I learned, well enough, how to read the weather, how to set the sails, how to navigate, how to anchor and weigh anchor, how to make our way along a difficult shore, how to stick with it, how to take the *Auk* out into a wind-strewn sea, how to bring her home, how to choose shelter for her. I could look up and read from the rigging what every stay and halyard was doing. But George never thought I could! What a sadness that is: the dream we both had at the beginning of the year, of a deepening friendship, of a trunk full of intimacies, of us becoming bound together, that never really developed.

Of course, he was right. If a halyard block broke in a storm, or the bilge pump blew; if the fuel supply to the engine became clogged, or if we were being blown, with no power, on to a lee shore, embayed and unable to escape, with a frightened crew around me, then I would have been at a loss. I simply did not have the hours, the days and the months for sea habits and sea knowledge to have been creased into my mind as they had been over years into his. Nor was I progressing fast enough. Too much time was spent away from the boat with the TV crew, filming various adventures underwater and down cliffs, chasing sheep and netting birds, digging up fossils or interviewing monks, for my sea knowledge to be deepened and enriched in the way it should have been. I was both a neglectful employer and a skiving pupil, arriving back at the boat from time to time, saying, 'Right. Everything OK? Let's go. Now. Aren't we ready? I know how to do it. Jump to. Tell me how. Why isn't this working? Haven't you mended that yet? What a mess it is down here. Help me. Listen to me. Don't talk to me like that. Let's try and have a good time, can we?' Inch by inch, yard by yard, over the weeks, George was improving and honing the *Auk*, and I can only imagine that in all of this, half there, half not there, half critical, half engaged, I was a nightmare.

I would not have put up with it for long, but I also saw, in miniature, we were acting out all the traditional sea dramas. We had rival authorities, which is always a mistake on a boat. He knew how to work things; I knew what I wanted to happen. He was, in a way, less certain than me; I was far less certain than him at sea. I was closely involved with making the TV programmes, George felt marginal to them, and when the TV crews came aboard he needed to impose his authority on them. Sometimes the world of the *Auk* felt bleak.

There were moments; of course there were more than moments. I will never forget the early summer morning he woke me, after sailing north all night from the Arans. We were in sight of the rocky, ironbound cliffs of High Island, the monastery island that once belonged to the Irish poet Richard Murphy, a place, as I had told George weeks before, I had long wanted to see. He had sailed five hours from midnight to bring us there. We were making towards it now in the dawn, over a swell that came and went, giving and withdrawing, the boat alive on the motion, as Murphy had written in 'Sailing to an Island':

The boom above my knees lifts, and the boat
Drops, and the surge departs, departs, my cheek
Kissed and rejected, kissed, as the gaff sways
A tangent, cuts the infinite sky to red
Maps, and the mast draws eight and eight across
Measureless blue . . .

In the early light, George took us deep into the lee of High Island's cliffs, so near that I could actually touch them from the deck of the *Auk*. But the walls were sheer and there was no way up on that side. 'High Island can never be possessed,' Murphy has written, 'because it will always remain in the possession of the sea.' So it was with us. We could not land and instead went on and on through the unforgettable morning that followed. George and Ben both lay below asleep and I sailed the boat, crossing the big sunlit bay between Inishbofin and Achill Island, filled with gratitude and – I will not shrink from this word – love for the two people asleep below, the sun over the mountains to the east of me, the headlands before me, a lovely big buffeting south-easterly blowing hard on my right cheek, a flat sea, all sails up, their canvas lit by the sun, shearwaters cruising past, the big, breaking sea my home.

On and on we strode northwards, past the Inishkeas, into the night, through Tory Island Sound, turning east there, making for Scotland, finding Islay coming up over the dawn horizon, sliding in along the wild and empty southern shore of Mull, finally coming in the evening into the Sound of Mull, where Sarah and the girls were waiting for us in a house on the shore. That is another all-life memorable moment. We had come three hundred miles nonstop – a night, a day, a night and a day – and George and I and Ben, all exhausted, all happy with the strength and sureness of the *Auk,* slid her towards the bay where Sarah was waiting. Stillness gathered on the grey waters and I remembered Auden's invocation of Evening, the calm, Athene-like goddess who hovers above our lives. 'Evening, grave, immense, and clear,' he calls,

> Overlook our ship whose wake
> Lingers undistorted on
> Sea and silence.

Molly and Rosie, my daughters, were standing in the shallows, the water up to their shins, the dogs further out, swimming out to us, the streams running down from the moorlands over the beach, the trees behind them, the lights in the house as yellow as apricots. It was an icon of home, of resolution and relief. In all of us, I realize, beneath the tensions and anxieties of life at sea, is that longing for home.

At heart, for George and me, there was little of home or homeliness in our sea relationship. The sadness of it was that, as we sailed on through the islands, we could both feel the other wishing for more, but could scarcely find a way through to it. I withdrew from the boat and its unresolvable tensions. A gap and something of a silence opened up between us. I made myself a passenger and allowed the boat to become George's place and George's world.

The most hidden recesses of the Hebrides became the most beautiful to me. I went abseiling down some cliffs one day with an Edinburgh botanist, William Milliken, looking for the big-leaved sorrel, the scurvy grass, and the wild carrots that grew there. We hung together in the shade of the cliff, a dank, lush place, with the sunlit Minch stretched out blue three hundred feet below us, a place, maybe, that no one had ever been before, and it felt like a kind of perfection, suspended between two worlds.

I went diving one morning in the kelp beds for the big pink sea urchins whose roe we ate for supper. In the small inflatable dinghy I fished for pollock and coaly in the tide riffles off the headlands and lowered creels for lobsters into the depths at the mouths of caves. These half-hidden corners felt like the real thing at the time, the places that resolved the enigma of arrival. But I see them now, in retrospect, as boltholes, away from the tensions I couldn't face.

One day out at St Kilda, away from the stamping mayhem of the ex-army camp there, its bar, the *Puff Inn*, and its busy people monitoring wild sheep or the missiles fired from the range on Benbecula, we went round to the other, ocean, side. The Atlantic-besieged cliffs of the St Kildan islands, visibly smashed and storm-swept up to two hundred feet above the surface of the sea, provide as enormous and powerful a meeting of rock and ocean as you ever find in Britain. In the looming, poised mass of the great sea-stacks, Stac an Armin and Stac Lee, and the bird-thick air around them, as dense with life in three dimensions as a field packed with corn, you feel nothing but the grandeur of the world.

The swell was pouring into the cave and breaking

among the big boulders in the hollow at the back. It was as if a beach had been buried deep in the socket of an eye. I rolled over the side of the boat and in, under, and down. The surge was there in the cave, swooping your body up towards the beach and back, a rocking, cradling motion, and I watched the surf from thirty feet below. Bubbles of air broke into the blue-grey world of stone and water, noiseless, the smoky opaqueness of underwater disturbed every few seconds by a sudden infusion of air, as if a gas cylinder was being released from above. We went down, three of us, forty or fifty feet into the depths of the cave. Secret St Kildan wonders! There was little kelp, only the vast, bare monumental walls of the underwater landscape, as big as Roman architecture, a drowned place, an Ice Age shore submerged by the Atlantic rising 10,000 years ago.

The surge of the sea animated it. The vertical cave walls, fifty yards long, sheer to sixty feet, were coated in clustered crowds of jewel anemones, purple, green, and silver. The crabs sat among them, alert and claws raised, hanging there poised, armed and Homeric, each one a toy Achilles with his spear and helmet set among the display cabinets in Cartier's or Tiffany's.

High above me, the glittery, silvered undersurface of the sea shifted in the swell. It was the most beautiful thing I had ever seen. Looking to one side, I saw a seal I hadn't noticed before, a sudden mammalian presence beside me in this exclusively mineral world, his hands wafting to and fro in front of his big liquid body. He approached to within a few feet. I saw the little dimples where his whiskers met his lip and his eyes looked straight and inquiring into mine. We gazed at each other. The air trapped in the pockets of his fur gave his whole bulk a blue, shimmery sheen as if encased in a singer's dress. He was sequinned from head to toe. His body was so full and rounded and so exotically liquid, and the dress so tight on his wonderfully moving, slow-dancing curves, that it seemed for a moment we were in the murky blue half-light of a nightclub somewhere and I was swimming with Shirley Bassey or Nina Simone, but in silence, all eyes and curiosity, a deep, careful 'Who are you?' emerging from those eyes. From us divers, little streams of bubbles rose to the surface as if from champagne. We had entered the seal's world. Two others came out from the shadows among the rocks and the three of them swam around us, a little frightening, because they might bite us, but at the same time mesmeric, so capable, turning in such perfect head-twisting curves, until at once they moved off together towards the shoal of pollock. But, because there is nowhere to hide in the sea, fish are quick and the pollock swam away in front of the seals, and we were left with nothing but the surge, the rocks, the wary, armoured crabs, and our own bespectacled, rubber-suited bodies, with our lumpen scuba gear and the bubbles coasting towards the air. I wished George had been down there too, but he was on the *Auk*, anchored in Village Bay.

It was like a marriage. We had arguments and apologies, long attempts to explain what each of us thought and deliberate, careful conversations to find out why the tension and gap existed between us. The difficulty kept recurring, particularly when I would turn up with the film crew and say 'Instant performance, please', at which George was expected to jump to it like a marionette, or when, just as suddenly, the circus would move off and leave him feeling abandoned. If ever, in some tiny way, he failed to deliver when required or made a demand when not required, it was as if he had stepped miles out of line.

At supper at the Indian restaurant in Stornoway one night, all of us deeply tired, George said that, for good sailing reasons, it would be better to go straight from the Hebrides to the Faeroes and then come back to Orkney, as the weather inevitably worsened towards the end of the year. In the prevailing winds, it would be a much more sensible way of doing it, wind on the port quarter up to the Faeroes, wind on the starboard beam back to Orkney. He knew of course that the film people wanted to do the journey in its real sequence, risking the difficulties of the end of the year, because 'exposure' was what, in the end, they wanted this to be about. 'None of you know what you are talking about,' George said. 'Do you have any idea what the North Atlantic is going to be like, or might be like, if it gets really bad?'

Will Anderson, the director, was all smiling deflection. He talked to Andrew Palmer, the executive producer, on the phone. Andrew was adamant that we should do things in the order in which they would appear on film: i.e. Orkney first, Faeroes second. I told George it was Andrew's call.

'No, no, no, no,' George said. 'You can't do it like that.'

'Oh, for God's sake,' I said, 'don't go and get high-horsy about this.'

'Do try and humour me, Adam,' George said slowly. 'I am paid to put in my pennyworth, my thruppence worth, and I simply ask it to be received with some courtesy.'

The formality was ominous. A crack had opened between us and everybody looked at their poppadoms.

'Listen,' I said, 'you have just to accept this as a normal, prosaic reality. We go from here to Orkney and from there to the Faeroes.'

'What do you mean "a normal, prosaic reality"? I don't know what those words mean. I don't understand what you are saying,' George said. So I repeated it in exactly the same, exaggeratedly plain words. George listened without response.

'I think you owe it to me to listen,' he said.

'I've listened to you,' I said, 'and we are going to do the journey in its natural sequence.'

'I think you'd have some trouble finding many professional skippers who would sit here and take this,' he said. That was undeniable, but it was the predicament we were in.

There may have been no answer to this. Perhaps

we were all simply edgy, unwilling to give ourselves over to each other, to any shared idea. Exhaustion may also have played its part. Or it may simply have been the problem of reconciling two divergent, equally demanding, and complex systems – the world of the boat and the world of the film – each with their fiercely insistent advocates, which could not, even with the patience of martyrs, have been easily reconciled. I belonged in both camps and felt treacherous to them both.

For whatever reason, the story is not neat, nor did it find a neat resolution. Things got better. We sang songs and got drunk. George and I reached a point where with scarcely a word we could indeed tack and wear the boat, bring her into harbour or away from a leeward quay, pick up moorings, trim the sails, be coherent in a difficult environment and sit there, at the end, below, warmly together, silent, no need for talk, a crew. How did that come about? I am not sure, but I do associate the easing of the tension with something that happened to us in Orkney, an event involving George, me, the *Auk* and a momentary sense of total and devastating relief, which was mysterious, disturbing, and entirely unexpected.

We had been for a few days on Stronsay. George had been staying on the boat and I had been living in one of the cells attached to a very strict, very conservative, and largely silent monastery on Papa Stronsay, a small island offshore. We had taken Orkney to heart: a sudden northern clarity after the damp, thick, peaty darkness of the Hebrides. It felt cleaner, lighter, harder and drier here. The air that September was like mountain air, as pure and as sharp. We'd had a wonderful day, streaming in on a southerly wind and an unruffled, slowly stirring sea, sailing over from Stornoway, past Cape Wrath, with the ice-scoured hills of Sutherland standing back away from the cape, the big lit swells coming up behind us like sofas on the move, and the long headlanded stretch of the north coast of Scotland lining out to the east, the seas breaking and creaming on to its empty shores.

At night, I would travel in my mind along the continuous thread of the *Auk*'s glittering path, dotted with my mistakes and muddles, our adventures and ecstasies, trailed out all the way around the rocky headlands, past the beaches and the green, cliffed islands, over the rolling widths of the sea, to what felt like the far, far distant south, a plane ride away but another world – a world before the *Auk* had entered it.

Something by D. H. Lawrence, which I read one night in that monastery, struck me. It was part of his book on America and American literature, but it came at me with force that night. 'Men are free,' Lawrence wrote,

> when they belong to a living, organic, believing community, active in fulfilling some unfulfilled, perhaps unrealised purpose. Not when they are escaping to some Wild West. The most unfree souls go West and shout of freedom. Men are freest when they are most unconscious of freedom. The shout is a rattling of chains, always was.

It is only what every social critic and seer from Marx and William Morris onwards has said, but circumstances can speak more powerfully than words. Words need the right conditions for their meaning to emerge and I read this in my little cell as if hearing it for the first time. Had our whole journey been nothing but a rattling of chains? Were George and I somehow trapped in a mobile cage of disengagement, our very search for freedom and fulfilment denied by the means we were using to look for it? Was this the truth behind our tension? Was the *Auk* a prison?

The next day was our last in Orkney. The weather was mild and sunny, with light southeasterlies forecast, a perfect and easy ride to the loneliest of all the Atlantic islands, three hundred miles north by northwest of us. We were going to the Faeroes. The long, easy lines and the pale, bleached colours of Orkney looked like a benediction. I had been deeply impressed by the twenty-five monks of the Golgotha monastery. Even that name is a signal of something. They came here in 1999, settling on their uninhabited speck of grass and rock because it represented 'a desert in the ocean', the sort of place monks have always sought out, away from the temptations and distractions of the city, to be named not after a version of Paradise or Eden but Golgotha, the place of the skull.

It is as profoundly conservative a regime as you can imagine. Every moment of the day, from its beginnings at three in the morning, when the island generator is turned on in preparation for the first mass at 3.45, to its conclusion in silence at seven in the evening, sleep at eight, is tightly and exactly regulated.

There is no speaking at meals, nor in their preparation or washing up. Dishes are cleaned to the singing of Latin hymns. The two novices among the twenty-five are allowed no jam with their bread and must remain in silence at all times. Every mass is said in Latin, since these monks are traditionalist Catholics, excommunicated by the Vatican, whose modern liberal drift they have rejected. This is a place devoted not to freedom but to obedience, the sanctity of tradition and the ancient Rule, even at the cost of broken relations with the Holy See.

The monastery is still raw in its newness: the chapel, for all its icons and the enrichments of its Catholic imagery, is in a converted herring gutting shed, the refectory in an old cow barn. The brothers' cells, in one of which I had been staying, are two long rows of small single-storey buildings, which are for the moment a stark and strange new addition to the Orkney landscape.

The abbot or vicar-general, a fifty-year-old New Zealander, Father Michael Mary, an amused, intelligent man, full of energetic visions for his future, told me, quite unequivocally and with a steady look straight into the back of my eyes, that as an agnostic, who didn't believe that Jesus was God, I was going to hell. I said I didn't believe in hell either. 'You might as well say,' he said touching the table between us, 'that this is made of marshmallow. It isn't. It's wood and you can't deny the realities.'

For all this exactness, this holding to many precise details of a long monastic tradition, in which there is nothing like television or radio, no private property, where all clothes and possessions (except toothbrushes and underwear) are shared, there is an astonishing absence of harshness. The discipline creates an air of ease and generosity. There is even, extraordinarily, a kind of gaiety about the monastery, laughter in the cowsheds as the monks milk their small herd of Jersey cows; as they build a new tractor house down by the pier, their habits smeared in mud and cement; as the little monastery launch makes its way to and from the pier on Stronsay; or as the two monks who are learning the bagpipes practise, the notes wobbling and wailing out on the edge of the old walled fields.

Perhaps this is obvious enough: the commitment to tradition, the deep engagement with the exactness of a monastic way of life, liberates these men in their daily dealings with the world and other people. Father

Michael Mary said to me as we were walking to the monastery's own hermitage, away from the main buildings down on the shore, that 'you only have to pick up the tradition which is lying there beside you, unused on the ground, to find that it is living in your hand'. And that is exactly what it felt like: life from a stone. The *Auk* and the monastery, in other words, seemed to be opposed to each other: a desire for freedom against a desire for certainty; the rattled against the constructed cage; tension and distance against conviction and warmth.

Father Michael Mary and one of the monks, a smiling, red-bearded man, Brother Nicodemus, came to see George on the boat and he showed them everything for hours. When they had done, he asked them if they would come and bless the *Auk*. In the early afternoon, the community of monks arrived down on the quay. Father Michael Mary was dressed in the white alb and the scarlet and gold embroidered chasuble and stole of his office. George and I stood beside the monks as they gathered around us in their black habits. Will Anderson, Johann Perry, the cameraman, and Paul Paragon, the sound man, prepared to film, and the ceremony began. The men, led by Father Michael

Mary, started to sing their Latin hymns to us and to the *Auk*, as one of the brothers sprinkled holy water on her decks from a silver vessel, walking alongside her, sprinkling first at the stern, all through the cockpit, on to the side-decks, up by the mainmast, on to the foredeck and finally to her bow, while the seamless and beautiful hymns floated out over the boat, us, and the water. Phrases came drifting at me – 'Maria Stella Maris', 'Noah ambulante in diluvio', Jonah and Job, St Paul undergoing his great storm en route to Malta. Every person in the Christian tradition who had suffered at the hands of the sea, and was in need of protection from it, was summoned to our aid. All around us, their sonorous, unaccompanied, chanted voices swelled and encompassed us.

What is it about a blessing? The way it suddenly releases such a river of sadness? I felt an extraordinarily powerful grief rising up in me, waves of it, unexpected, unsummoned, unwanted. I looked across at George and saw him in a state of collapse, his face crumpled as if someone had punched him. My own tears came more as a kind of choking than anything else. I had to hold my face in my hands. I saw that Johann was crying. Why were we like this? It was not simply the beauty of the moment, although it was beautiful. Nor was it a matter of conversion or belief. None of us were 'getting God' that afternoon. In a way it was simpler than that. We were weeping, I think, because, for once in all our lives, a strong hand, the hand of tradition, embodied by these people we scarcely knew, believing things we did not believe, seemed to be coming up beneath us, broad enough to carry us, broad enough even to gather the battered, stalwart *Auk* in its folds, and, having taken us up like that, was now pouring a blessing over us. It was as if, in an act of powerful theatre, that tradition of strictness and self-abnegation to which these men had devoted their lives had become, for a moment, fatherly to us, in a way that, grown men as we were, ever required to be self-sufficient and upright in the world, we had not known for many years. It was, in other words, an act of sustaining love. Father Michael Mary gave me a rosary and Brother Nicodemus gave George the rosary from around his own neck. Neither of us could speak.

We went aboard, cast off, hoisted the sails, and started to move away from the quay. The Golgotha brothers resumed their Latin hymns, the wind began to fill our sails, and, as we sheeted in, the *Auk* began to gather way, making with great certainty for the open sea, as if she had borrowed something from the place she had just left. 'We won't forget that,' I said to George.

'No,' he said, 'we won't.' He hugged me, and I hugged him too.

8

The Arrival

The *Auk* finally raised the Faeroes late in the afternoon. Autumn was verging into winter. The passage
had begun sweetly enough, but, as a low had come
through, the wind had veered and stiffened, and the
boat had been sailing close-hauled most of the day,
well heeled over, only a reefed main and the stays'l
up. Now there was snow. Grey, twisting showers of
it were coming out of the northwest like smudges on
the wind. When they arrived, the air bit into the skin
of the face as if filled with knives. Drifts of the granular
snow were piling up in the ridges of our hats and sat
in small cushions in the corners of the cockpit. It was
soft-looking air that hurt. Anyone on the helm needed
a scarf wrapped around their face, but the *Auk* was
in fine fettle, her deck stripped, clean and exact, and
George, as ever, was cooking something down below.

Land comes up grey and indistinct, a suggestion of what it might be rather than an announcement of what it is. It is always taught to novice navigators that the object you are in charge of is not a boat but 'a circle of uncertainty'. Too many forces are working on you – the leeway, or drift downwind, the shifting tides, the inattention of the helmsman, perhaps the inaccuracy of the compass, even misreading the charts – for you ever to be sure of where you are. At sea, unless you know where you are, you can't know where you are. And the further you have come from the last point at which you were certain, your circle of uncertainty grows with every passing mile.

It is a powerful idea, a sea metaphor worthy of the *Odyssey*: you travel on, you attend to every knot and sheet in the boat as best you can; you trim the sails, you read the sea, you ride its sudden surges, you slew away down the slopes it provides; you work with your companions, you learn who they are as they learn who you are; and all the time, all around you, the circle of uncertainty grows. After a day or two, you are navigating a balloon towards your destination. Nor do you know in which part of it you are living. Are you on its leading edge, or its wings? Or are you trailing far behind?

It is tempting and flattering to think you are in the centre of your circle, that you are, pretty well, where your calculations put you, and that the circle of uncertainty is just a construct devised by the over-cautious to discipline the free. But the circle of uncertainty is the hardest fact you have. The haziness of your condition is not helped by the difficulty of reading the land from the sea. Even from a few miles out, land shows little of its nature. There is scarcely any colour in the shore and the forms of the coast are flattened. Headlands and bays merge into a single canvas-thin backdrop. In that way, the circle of uncertainty is not resolved by landfall, but dramatised by it. It has never been wider. You are days away from the last moment of real knowledge and now the land confronts you with its questions. What am I? Am I what you think I am? Where does this shore welcome, and where does it threaten? And don't interpret me in the way that would be most convenient. Expect the worst, stay alert, treat me with the suspicion I deserve.

As the grey shapes thickened and darkened, the Faeroes announced themselves in blank-faced, un-interrogatable simplicity. Stark, black, volcanic basalts, sheet after sheet of them, one on top of another, preserve the sequence of the vast eruptions which made these islands fifty million years ago. The guts of the earth spat the Faeroes out and the Atlantic is now doing its best to level them. Black rock, grey ocean and, between those two brutalities, a skin of green, the colour of life. It is a naked landscape, almost exactly the same in every part, a two-phase drama on display in front of you – eruption then destruction – with a brief interval, between the two, of life staking its claim.

Night fell while we were still at sea and the wind picked up another notch. We were making for Tórshavn on Streymoy, Thor's harbour, the place where the Thunderer could rest, and we were now reaching north on a big westerly. The islands are sliced by deep, sharp-sided glacial fjords and sounds, through which the Atlantic winds and tides drive with a force rarely matched further south. The Faeroes are like a giant sieve placed across the tidal streams of the ocean, and those streams, forced through the gaps, are Amazons and Mississippis for weight and strength of water on the move.

As we approached them in the evening, longing as ever for arrival, the relationship of sea and land began

to shift. When the tide runs, it is not in fact the water that moves. The bulge of water that the moon and the sun's gravitational pull creates on each side of the earth remains pretty well where it is. The movement is of the solid, rocky earth inside that stretched envelope of the ocean. So it isn't the tide that is moving: it is the earth revolving within its skin of water. As we neared the huge black bulk of the Faeroes at night, with a powerful westerly wind coming over them towards us, and an equally powerful west-going tide pulling us into the channels and gaps between the islands, it was not difficult to think that the islands were heading towards us. The tidal atlas for the Faeroes shows deep, ragged red flags of turbulence in the mouths of the sounds, around the headlands and tailing out for many miles into the Atlantic on either side. In the presence of these huge, planetary forces, what was the *Auk* but a bobbing piece of flotsam? The islands were coming for us like a herd of bison.

Our journey had never seemed so elemental as this, nor the Atlantic world so animated, so *animal*. As we crossed the mouth the wide channel between Suðuroy, the southernmost of the Faeroes, and the islands to the north of it, that tidal stream dragging

us westwards, that enfolding of the great black batlike cloak of the Faeroes around us, suddenly became more intense. The wind had the *Auk* well over. The whole of her leeward side-deck was awash. The water was up on the coach house roof and, from below, the glass of the coach house windows was filled with the Atlantic, mesmerisingly strange at night, that gushing runnel of water, no more than a quarter of an inch of glass away, lit from inside like a model of natural violence.

Entranced by this night scene, I clipped my harness on to the lifeline and went to sit on the foredeck as we plunged through the dark. Everything was high energy: the sea around us, driven one way by the tide, the other by the shrieking wind, was standing in peaks and ridges that were breaking on the spot. The *Auk*, for all her surging progress through the water, was scarcely making headway over the ground. Looking to see how we were doing by measuring the apparent speed at which one headland crossed another, or a distant piece of land disappeared behind a nearer – taking transits, as it is called – it was perfectly clear that the islands and their tide-rivers had us in their grip. A hellish kind of adrenaline thrill. I sat down below, trying to work out with the charts, the tide

tables, and the tide atlas what would happen if we could not escape the grasp of these west-going tides; if, even with the engine on at full throttle, the hold of the Faeroes, its magical and invisible fingers – the turning of the earth itself – would pull us in and swallow us, some kind of northern Homeric fate, as if this were Charybdis and Calypso combined. It felt like the sea of fate.

The figures were clear enough: if the tide could not be beaten, we could go with it, allow ourselves to be swept through the Sound between Skúvoy and Sandoy and then, in five or six hours, as the tide turned, we would be swept back in with it, north of Sandoy and up to Tórshavn.

That sounds like a neat bit of geography, riding the earth as the earth needs to be ridden. But it failed to take account of one thing: the wind. It had veered again into the northwest and was coming at us in lumps, gusted and broken in the lee of the tall islands. One of the gusts, its arrival invisible in the dark, drove the *Auk* further over than she had ever been. Books, pans, and possessions went scattering all over the cabin below. I found myself, for a moment, standing vertically on the lowest part of the mizzenmast, the entire world of the *Auk* turned through what must have been sixty or seventy degrees. Then she came back up again and on we plunged. No damage except to the anemometer at the very head of the mainmast, whose revolving cups and arms had been swept away. We now had no idea how hard the wind was blowing.

There was no way we could head into a wind like that, and so our predicament was set. We were held for the time being almost fixed between wind and tide, as if between the finger and thumb of the Atlantic world, the boat, and all of us, under immense strain, the seas breaking white on the dark headlands a mile or two to the west, but, for all the rush and violence, immobile.

It was wonderful, a savage spectacle in bitter monochrome. I had never been in such a place, held as if gravity-free, but so brutally subject to the world, to its wind and waters. The Vikings thought hell was cold, 'the cave of sharp thorns, a cold, wet hollow where even the water is bitter'. But was anywhere so hellish and so heavenly as this? At once? I said as much to George, but he didn't like it.

The engine was not happy. Its note had changed and George guessed, as turned out to be the case, that when it was running with the boat heeled over so far in the gusts, it had sucked a dose of seawater in through the leeward diesel breather pipe, whose mouth is only just above deck level. The fuel was probably contaminated now and the engine was labouring. If it failed out here, and if the rig broke and left us without motive power, then the tide would surely set us on to the headlands, no place for any talk of magnificence or spectacle. I stood corrected, my excitement from then kept private, my love of all this silent.

Perhaps that too is an Atlantic lesson. If you are to exist in these wild places, then you must be both George and me: relish the totality, give yourself over to the magnificence of this world and, at the same time, resist and control it. In other words, both submit and deny. Neither is good enough without the other.

We read the instruments and gauged the transits. The strength of the tide was due to fall over the evening and eventually, before midnight, to turn in our direction. Very slowly, our speed over the ground began to climb. We could reduce the revs of the engine. The lighthouses guarding the entrance to Tórshavn Sound began to beckon us in. Finally, just before midnight, the lights of the port itself came clear of the headland to the south of them. We were out of the tide grip and making for safety. Harbour lights! Our final landfall, at last, tying up between the Faeroese boats in the inner harbour, exhausted after another dance with the Furies.

Even as we arrived in the Faeroes, it was clear that the time had come to go home. The week or so we spent in the islands was overshadowed by the winter. The snow had already come to lie on the tops of the hills. The Faeroese themselves stood with their hands in their pockets on the quaysides and clucked their tongues at us. *Where* had we come from? Where? A Cornish boat? At this time of year? It could be windy in the Faeroes. And did we know about the tides?

But, for all that, there was no wagging of fingers. The Faeroese are seamen of the most self-reliant kind. There are no lifeboats in Faeroese harbours, because 'we don't want to rely on an organization to save us. If we are out fishing and someone is in trouble, we'll go and help him ourselves.' They have made this Arctic frontier of the North Atlantic their own. They make a fortune out of the cod and haddock in the spectacularly rich grounds their 200-mile fishing limit encloses.

The islands' GNP is over £1 billion a year, just

over 80 per cent of that coming from the fish. One morning, when we were in the northern boomtown port of Klaksvik on Bordoy, a trawler came in after only ten days out on the Faeroes Bank, carrying 100 tons of cod, worth £180,000, and paying each of the twenty crew £5,500 for their ten days' work. Klaksvik was full of fishing stories: boats taking so much fish that they have sunk under the weight of their own catch; another, a rather rusty second-hand trawler from Hull, going down a few years ago when the weight of fish actually broke through the bottom of the hull.

Can you imagine, after all George and I had struggled through in the course of the year, how extraordinary this atmosphere seemed? All year we had been on an impoverished edge, which was drawing what life it had from the exigencies and difficulties of its existence. Out here in the wildest province the North Atlantic could provide, after such a hair-raising arrival, we had come to a world of over-brimming wellbeing. In Tórshavn, little wooden cafés, smelling of apple and cinnamon, served Viennese cakes and cups of dense, rich coffee. The boatyard on the south side of the inner harbour was run with a photocopier-level of efficiency – no rubbish, no fuss, no rusty, macho heroics, just acres of clean, businesslike, swept concrete and men getting on with it. This wasn't some raw, exposed outermost place. It was its own middle.

We went catching fulmars on Kalsoy in the far north of the archipelago; we went digging coal with handpicks at Hvalba on Suðuroy; we went catching sheep on Koltur with Bjørn Patursson, the one farmer still living on that island, teetering with him along a cliff path in pursuit of the rams he had put out on the most exposed flank of cliffside pasture he could find. He had brought along his friends and cousins, and his nephew, who farmed the other side of a tide-ripped channel at Kirkjubøur on Streymoy, where the Paturssons had farmed at least since the mid-sixteenth century. All of them had arrived on Streymoy by helicopter, a subsidised service for remote island farmers who wanted to gather their sheep. Bjørn's son-in-law, an engineer on an oil support boat in the Gulf of Benin, now on leave, told me how a farmer on the neighbouring island of Hestur had been gathering sheep on a path like this a few years ago and had slipped. Half of him had been found in the sea and half on the rocks. We talked about seabirds. 'There's nothing I love more than a Manx shearwater,' I said.

'Yes, delicious, aren't they?' the handsome engineer said. And we all slaughtered the big, rough-woolled rams with Bjørn that evening, a captive bolt to the head as he held the animals in his arms. Tears came into his eyes as the first of them died, 'because it is that time of year, and I cannot help thinking of all the years past when I do this'.

I wanted to be Faeroese! Everything I had hoped for from the Atlantic world seemed to come to fruition here. We were in our last few days but we had landed in the place I had wanted to be all year. The islands had neither died, in the way so much of the west coast of Scotland has died, nor been reinvaded and yuppified as so much of southwest Ireland has been. The ways of being on the Faeroes, which had always sustained people here, of fishing and fowling, of raising sheep and cattle, of making extraordinarily warm, dry, and comfortable, turf-roofed houses, even of knitting jerseys and building small wooden boats – all this was alive here in a way it simply is not further south.

The living survival of habits of mind, more than any ancient technology, is what drew me. The Faeroese think that the more extreme the conditions an animal has been subjected to, the tastier the meat. Hilltop flesh is better than the soggy stuff from the seaside; remote island flesh better than the wide open pastures of Streymoy; best of all is mutton from the sort of near-vertical 'garden', as he described it, in which Bjørn had kept his young rams all year. The Faeroese continue to chase and eat the wild things that the rest of Europe has become too squeamish to countenance. Puffins, fulmars, guillemots, pilot whales, even dolphins, form a steady part of the Faroese diet, not as some fetishistic return to the life-giving properties of wild food but 'because they are delicious', as Bjørn said, which they are.

What was I after here? What did I envy in them? Everything! Their smiling, skilful relaxation as they danced their way along the tiny, sometimes slippery cliff path we took to collect the rams, which I and the film crew crept along as if we were within an inch of our lives (as we were); the unaffectedly serious and respectful way in which they treated the animals they were preparing to slaughter; their uncomplicated hospitality; their knowledge that their families had owned and farmed the same hillsides for many centuries, not, as it might be further south in Europe, as grounds for rather fat complacency, but for a sort of tough-minded confidence and brio; the combination of calculation and breeziness that means that houses are only built in those places where boulders from the fast-eroding ridge-tops will not crush them, and yet which decides to paint them in the most expressive fishing-boat colours; which lays out the long-lines to catch cod in the most precise and delicate ways on the seabed, and then decides to sit up and play cards all night because 'sleep is for old men'. The Faeroese, in other words, combine precision – Switzerland is not tidier – and gusto, daring and kindness, an understanding of the violence and difficulty of their environment, with a kind of panache and showmanship, *and* a phlegmatic calm, all of which makes them the great seamen they are. Maybe, I wondered, this is what the Vikings were like. Were these the qualities that conquered the world?

Or perhaps there is something broader at work here. This is exactly how nineteenth-century visitors used to describe the St Kildans, dancing down their 1,000-foot cliffs on horsehair ropes with as much abandon as most of us can manage on a bicycle, laughingly living on an edge that would terrify others. It is not now, though, a set of qualities you find in those parts of Atlantic Britain from which the population has drained away over the last 150 years. Why is that? Why has the vitality remained in the Faeroes that has largely evaporated from other North Atlantic islands?

There may be a political-cum-historical explanation. The Faeroes are a unique case. Although their population and language are largely derived from Norway, a series of historical accidents has meant they are politically subject to Denmark. The Faeroese's idea of themselves disconnects them at heart from the country into which they might otherwise have retreated. To be Faeroese is to be, in your essence, independent and self-sufficient, not reliant on some big, powerful centralised market to the east and south but to be thriving, coherent, and well, out here, a thousand miles away in mid-Atlantic. This is where they are. Remote from where?

Life on the Faeroes is not antique or nostalgic. All farmers are on the Internet. The ferries are full of shiny new BMWs and Mercedes. The cod-processing factory in Klaksvik is as sleek and neat as any in the world, producing *goujons de cod* or boxes full of ready-to-sell stockfish for anywhere in the world that wants it. The Faeroes, in other words, are not living in the past, but importantly they haven't abandoned it either. Sheep, for example, are not sent to some central abattoir-cum-wholesaler to be slaughtered and sold. They are killed, and eaten, on the farm where they grew up, something that is now illegal in the rest of Europe. Men continue to be both farmers and fishermen here, in a way that was once universal on the Atlantic margin but has now almost entirely disappeared under the pressures of professionalisation.

That perfectly real, and often clearly difficult, combination of the inherited and the current made me love the place. The Faeroes didn't get to me emotionally, in the way that the monks of the Golgotha monastery had done; nor give me the moments of ecstasy that Skellig Michael had; nor seem as intriguingly and disturbingly powerful as the figure of Hervé Mahe in Port Magee. But the Faeroes felt rather better and even healthier than those strange extremes had done. The Faeroes, if only I had been Faeroese, would have been for me what they are for the Faeroese – that strange and beautiful thing: a wild Atlantic home, filled with women, children, schools, home, homeliness; and with wildness, bravura, excitement, an incredibly abundant wildlife, and a perfectly straightforward relationship

to it, neither destructive nor over-reverential, but energetic, optimistic, confident, healthy, and alive. Everything you might hope for from home you can find
there; as well as everything you might hope for from
the wild. I don't know anywhere like it, and it now
floats in my mind as a kind of dream.

If the monks of Golgotha have any influence on
these things I would ask them simply to pray for this:
would God please bring me, and all those I love, back
as Faeroese? But I know they don't, he won't and that
the world does not work like that. Perhaps, in the end,
we are all removed from the lives we would like to
lead, emigrants and exiles to a man.

9

Seamanship

The end was wrong, though. Our arrival in Tórshavn
had done damage to the *Auk*. The battens had been
torn out of both the mizzen and the mains'l on that
wild night when we had been caught in the tide. The
gulps of seawater which the engine had sucked in had
not done any good at all. While I had been gallivanting
around the Faeroes with the film crew, relishing my
arrival, fowling and fishing, tucking into my pilot
whale stew, George had been buried in the harbour
trying to get the boat sorted and the sails repaired.
The steering system seemed to have developed a fault
too: when you turned the wheel to port the rudder
would sometimes respond and sometimes not, a
hydraulic problem whose cause wasn't clear. Even at
the last, the wholeness George and I had both wanted
from this journey was as far away as it had ever been.

I was having fun, he was in the engine room. I would arrive back at the boat saying 'Hi!', he would look up wearily from the bilges after two or three frustrating hours, trying to get a nut on to a bolt in a corner which you could scarcely reach and could not see.

The weather had been vicious, welding-torch blasts of cold arctic wind burning between the islands for a week. It had meant we had stayed almost twice as long as intended. Sarah was anxious for me to come home. It had all gone on too long. One of the children was ill, the dog had run away, her business had entered one of its periodic phases of acute stress. I had to come home.

I had wanted nothing more than to sail back with George to England. Without the other pressures of film-making, it would have been a mending passage. But if I had waited to come home with him, after the work had been done on the *Auk*, and the weather, which was forecast gales for days, had cleared, I wouldn't have been home for the best part of two weeks. I had to fly. We left George and the *Auk* in Tórshavn. She looked lovely tied up at the quay, riding much higher than the little Faeroese boats around her, dressed, at least in my mind, in the adventures she'd had, anxious, like a dog at the door, for another go. George looked and felt bereft, abandoned by us all after he had done everything for us.

Jacky Houdret, the indefatigable Keo producer, put an ad on Faeroese radio, asking if any seamen would like to crew a sailing boat back to England. About a dozen turned up at the quayside, George picked one and within a few days the two of them set off south in fine conditions. Twelve days and 1200 miles later, George and the *Auk* were back in Falmouth.

This was not the right end. George and I should have been casting off together in Tórshavn, heading south, reeling up the cotton thread that we had been slowly unwinding all year. At home with Sarah, as George and the *Auk* made their way south, I thought of that every day. We were texting each other. I knew at almost every moment where he was. The *Auk* and he were running over the ground of our shared, or at least part-shared, year.

I had the chart of the northeast Atlantic on my wall, reaching from Brittany to Iceland and southern Norway. I could look at it and see a band of it, a sailed swathe of ocean, glowing with memories, a lit arc of life and richness draped around the western boundaries of the British Isles. A stretch of country, which I had only known remotely and patchily before, now had a shape and a continuity. I could see it all, from one headland to another, and could bring it all to mind. It had come to occupy me, as if I had grown another lobe.

Memory is the imagination's cousin and as I sat in my room again, looking at that chart, I was reading the same pages I had been looking at a year before, but a richer, illuminated version of them, sequined with marvels in a way they had not been before. The pale-skinned beauty of the Scillies at the spring equinox, as the tide dropped away and revealed a sun-drenched, sand-thickened Bronze Age landscape; the whales in the Sound of Sleat lunging that still evening like sea-mastiffs after the shoals of sprats; the tall, canted pyramids of the St Kilda stacks standing like black totems on the western horizon as the sun dropped behind them; the shearwaters all year, signalling to me freedom and excellence; the Romanesque, sea-cliff substance of St Magnus, the red sandstone cathedral in Kirkwall, the church at the heart of the North Atlantic world; the casual grace of the Faeroese fulmar-catchers, smilingly relaxed as they plucked the birds from the wind.

These are treasures that can never be denied and will never go away. I now own them. George and the *Auk* acquired them for me and they exist in a kind of everlasting present, a strange echo of what he said to me as we left Falmouth for Ireland that dark evening. Wherever I am, or George is, whatever we are doing, those shearwaters are cutting their curves above the breaking seas; those whales are sliding their long dark backs under the shoals of prey; and the fulmars are fluttering, caught in the tall, delicate nets of their hunters. That is the treasure-hoard of a journey like this: a collection of memories through which, for ever, you can riffle your hand, as though through the hair of a child.

Memories like that cannot be shared. Worse, they actively set you apart from those who did not share the experience. Sarah was shut away when I came home. It had been too much. She knew, and I knew, that she could not ask where I had been and what I had done. She had protected herself and our children by withdrawal. That wasn't a process which could be flicked into reverse when I returned. I knew that, and for a while we simply lay alongside each other, like two boats berthed, co-present but not co-terminous, together and apart. It was all right, like a new meeting between us, or at least a meeting again, going quietly and carefully, a slow and courteous unpeeling of layers.

I wanted to be at home and with her, more than ever and more than I have ever wanted anything. That is also what the journey had taught me: the womanly beauty of homeliness. The Egyptian hieroglyphs for woman and for home are the same, and that enfolding and absorption is what I knew, on returning, I both needed and needed to support. Life was not out with the boys; life was here with women and children.

Within a few days, I pushed a knife into this. The TV company needed more film of George and me at sea in rough weather. They wanted to have us at the end of a hard, short-handed two- or three-day passage, all gaiety gone, sick and dead with it. I went to tell Sarah. She was upstairs in the bedroom by the window, the cold white light of November falling on her face. She started to cry, her face in her hands, that white November light. 'We've all held on,' she said. 'It's been a long time. And you can't keep adding to it. Every time you add to it, it gets worse and worse.' Her face and shoulders were held away from me, rounded into themselves like the shell of an egg.

This was the other side of my encounter with the seal in the cave at St Kilda. Why, for God's sake, look for intimacy with a seal, if the price of doing that is these shoulders turned away, this face held in these hands, this woman sobbing beside me?

She told me about a bad moment in her year. It was midsummer. I was in Ireland somewhere. The fields at home were filled with flowers and new grasses. She had decided to take the children out into the fields to camp for a night or two, 'to get our sea,' she said, 'something at home of what you were getting out there.' They'd had a lovely time, cooking on the fire beside the tents, watching the moon come up over the buttercup meadows. It was some consolation in a time that was bogged down in work and business.

The next evening, they thought they would do it again and walked back out into the fields with their campfire supper and bottles of lemonade. Someone had let cows into the meadow during the day. They had trampled all over the tents and destroyed them. The canvas was torn, the poles were bent and every-thing inside was broken and wrecked. They had all trailed home feeling broken too. If I'd been there, simply as another person, another source of energy, it would have been all right. But I wasn't, so it wasn't. I needed to be here. I needed to love them, not in some distant, airy-fairy way, but in the practicalities of mending the tent and keeping the cows in the right field. Other echoes came back to me. Wasn't this what George had said to me over and over again? That it was all very well sitting on deck looking at the view while someone else worried about the engine and all the other systems by which the boat worked, but loving the view had nothing to do with seamanship. Seamanship was keeping other people alive.

George and Kathy came to stay in December and we four talked into the night about the polarities of our year, our separations, the ways we had and hadn't been with each other. I began to say to George the burden of what I have written here. We felt our way carefully, each testing the other to see how much we could say, like doctors pressing on a tender stomach. By the fire, with the candles lit, I thanked him for the months of care he had devoted to me and the *Auk* and our journey, something to which he had given, I thought, more than he had received.

'I can't say what went wrong, Adam,' he said. 'Perhaps it was the teaching thing. It's a very curious art and I know I struggle with it. I have always worked in a world where not losing the dinghy over the side has been the proof of a good job. It didn't have to be achieved in a caring, patient way.'

'You mean when you asked me to lash the dinghy and you kicked it to show it was loose?'

'Yes,' he said. 'The irony is that you remember me kicking the dinghy, don't you? Not that we didn't lose the dinghy over the side?'

'I would rather we had lost the dinghy. Or neither. I'd rather you'd shown me how to do it.'

'I know. I was tired. And I never did show you how to do that knot.'

'No.'

'Though you asked me several times.'

'No.'

'This is about seamanship, Adam. And seamanship is about taking and carrying the risk. The Risk with a capital R. I was hired to look after the boat. That was my job. If something had gone wrong, if someone had died, it wouldn't have been you they came to. I would have been the person standing there. You're a plucker, Adam.'

'A what?'

'You float above things, you float from one thing to another, you take life's pleasures as if they were designed to please you. You pluck. It's an enviable condition. It's the luckiest place a man could find. But it doesn't carry the risk, does it? That was always with me. I carried it for week after week, second-guessing the next thing to go wrong. You never shared it, you never came in there with me.'

'I think it is probably impossible to share that,' I said.

'I have never not shared it before. And there were times, like that night of the big tide off the Faeroes, when I kept thinking to myself, "Come on, Adam, help me, come in here too. Don't just keep saying how fantastic the waves are." But you never did. And because you never took the risk, the risk always came between us.'

'But we're all right now,' I said.

'Yes, we are,' George smiled. 'We followed our course, we came back, we're all in one piece. We rubbed each other up the right way and the wrong way. And no one can say we don't know each other more deeply because of it. That's a rare thing, and you and I will never lose it. A small piece of my life is welded to yours.'

'Yes,' I said, '– welded – that's right, and mine to yours.'

Sarah, George and Kathy sat at the table, the candles glittering up into their eyes and teeth. It was a harbour picture, a painting of home. What was seamanship? Keeping other people alive.

I went out in the night and lay down on the cold December grass. A clear sky. I looked at the stars. Seamanship? What was it? Attention to detail; nurturing the ship; resourcefulness; and, more importantly, an ability to catch a kettle before it falls and to look after people and things before they need it. Did I have that? Could the plucker sail? I gazed at the stars and hardly knew.

Acknowledgements

I owe more than I can say to the many people who became part of the *Auk* and her voyage during 2003. It was both a privilege and a huge pleasure to be with and work with the team of resourceful, energetic, warm and generous people who made the Channel 4/ National Geographic series for Keo Films and ushered the *Auk* along her way. They were: Directors: Lucy Sandys-Winsch, Nick Read, Will Anderson, Andrew Palmer and Ben Roy; Producers: Ben Roy and Jack Houdret; Camera: Steve Standen, Luke Cardiff, Richard Hill and Johann Perry; Sound: Ian Maclagan, Paul Paragon, Simon Farmer, and Godfrey Kirby; Editors: Simon Beeley and Peter Cartwright; and in the Keo office: Jon Hubbard, Katherine Perry, Claire Hamilton, Toyin Ogunbiyi and Ewan Fletcher.

*   *   *

I would like especially to thank Will Anderson, Zam Baring and Andrew Palmer for their friendship, for sticking with the idea long after all others would have dropped it and for shepherding me so carefully along so many dodgy paths.

Susan Watt at HarperCollins has been my guide and mentor for many years, for which I will always remain enormously grateful. My agent Caroline Dawnay at Peters, Fraser and Dunlop, and her assistant Alex Elam, continue to do everything any author could hope for, for which, as ever, all thanks.

My heartfelt love and thanks to George Fairhurst, the *Auk*'s skipper, for putting up with me for a year, for taking the *Auk* where no other skipper would have dared, for doing every single thing that was asked of him in the most difficult circumstances, for the warmth of his friendship and for taking the candour of these pages in the spirit in which they were intended.

Above all, my love and gratitude to Sarah Raven, whose own love does not alter when it alteration finds.